French Chic

QUILTING
PATCHWORK
AND APPLIQUE

100 IDEES

BALLANTINE BOOKS · NEW YORK

Conceived, designed and produced by
Conran Octopus Limited
28-32 Shelton Street
London WC2 9PH

Managing Editor: Jasmine Taylor
Contributing Editor: Hilary More
Art Editor: Caroline Pickles
Editor: Diana Mansour
Illustrators: Cooper West, Peter Meadows

The editors would like to thank Beryl Miller for making the cover
background.

Library of Congress Catalog Card No: 85-91566

ISBN 345-33610-0

Manufactured in Hong Kong

First American Edition: September 1986

10 9 8 7 6 5 4 3 2 1

Acknowledgments (Photographer/Stylist)

10-17 Marcel Duffas/J. Schoumacher   19-20   MacLean/C. Lebeau/J. Schoumacher
21   J. Tisné/I. Garçon   23   G. de Chabaneix/C. Lebeau   25   G. de Chabaneix/C. Lebeau
27-28   B. Maltaverne/C. Lebeau   31   J. Tisné/I. Garçon
33   G. de Chabaneix/C. de Chabaneix   37   Y. Duronsoy/Jacobs
39   J. Dirand/C. Lebeau   42-45   G. Bouchet/C. Lebeau   47   Godeaut/C. Lebeau
50-51   M. Duffas/J. Schoumacher   53-56   G. de Chabaneix/C. de Chabaneix/Jacobs
57   B. Maltaverne/C. Lebeau   58-63   A. Bianchi/I. Garçon
65   G. de Chabaneix/J. Shoumacher   69-75   G. de Chabaneix/I. Garçon
77-79   B. Maltaverne/C. Lebeau

CONTENTS

INTRODUCTION

Although they have the image of crafts which require specialist skills and painstaking effort, patchwork, quilting and appliqué are based on simple and straightforward sewing skills and can be great fun.

Whether you already have some experience or are a complete beginner, you are likely to find that your only difficulty lies in choosing which one of the numerous entertaining and attractive projects you are going to start with.

Children will adore the dinosaur sleeping bags, and though complex-looking they are much easier to sew than you would imagine. The surface is supposed to resemble wrinkled reptilian skin – which is ideal if you are a novice quilter.

If you want to embark on a smaller project there are plenty of other things to make for children, ranging from a tote bag shaped like a horse's head, to charming appliqué motifs of squirrels to be stitched on to bought clothes. Or you might like to make the quick-and-easy child's quilt – it uses a speedy technique of tacking-size stitches with tufted intersections for a quilted cover that could be assembled in just a few hours.

If, on the other hand, you are looking for something more sophisticated, you may be tempted to make the white-on-white window blind, the Japanese-style tablecloth or the quick but very stylish patched curtains. Those who like traditional work, but with a slightly unusual twist to it, will appreciate the Irish blanket, which is made with warm tweeds instead of the more common cotton fabrics; or perhaps you would prefer the Seminole patchwork. This looks enormously complicated, but it is made with a clever strip-patchwork technique, stitched by machine, that greatly reduces the work involved in making this apparently intricate cover.

For those who enjoy embroidery, there are several projects that offer a chance to display decorative stitches, such as the Victorian crazy cover, where the patches can be embroidered in place, or the white linen hanging, with satin stitch initials.

So if you have always imagined that patchwork was a matter of sewing endless hexagons together by hand, that appliqué was too elaborate, or that quilting was strictly the preserve of little old ladies who had learned the skill from their mothers before them, now is the time to change your ideas and learn how versatile and stylish these crafts can be.

BASIC ESSENTIALS

The techniques used in quilting, patchwork and appliqué are all very straightforward and the path to success is to make templates as accurate as possible and to follow through each stage methodically and neatly. In essence, however, the sewing skills used are just the same as those needed for dressmaking. Although the instructions generally state whether a piece should be stitched by hand or machine, most of them could be made by either method, provided you use the right kind of template and/or sewing techniques.

Color variations

There is no reason why the colors suggested for the designs in this book should not be changed to suit your decor or your clothes, and in fact it is not always possible to find the same or similar colors as shades go in and out of fashion.

Sometimes, however, a change of color can alter the appearance of a design, particularly in the case of patchwork, which depends for its effect on a good contrast of colors and light and dark tones. If you are thinking of using a different selection of colors, the best way to check that your idea will work is to make a small-scale copy of the design, with no colors filled in; take several tracings, and then experiment with a succession of different color variations, using felt tipped pens or crayons.

Another method, which is particularly useful if you are not sure whether a blend of patterned fabrics will work well together, is to make a small-scale outline of the design and then cut fabric patches, to this scale and without seam allowances. Place the patches on the paper and you will have at least a fairly good idea of how well they will work together when the patches are scaled up to the full size.

Enlarging a design

The designs given in this book can easily be enlarged to the correct size. If the design is already on a square grid, simply copy it, square for square, on to a grid of the correct finished size. Dressmakers' pattern paper can be used for this or, for smaller designs, ordinary graph paper. The most accurate way to copy is to mark each place where the lines of the design cross the lines of the large grid and then to join up these marks.

If the design in the book is not already on a grid, simply draw a squared grid on tracing paper, place this over the image which you wish to copy, using masking tape at the corners, then trace off the image and enlarge it as already described.

Transferring a design

In cases where the designs are embroidered as well as appliquéd, it will be necessary to transfer the design directly to the fabric. The simplest way to do this is to use carbon paper. Choose dressmakers' carbon paper, which is available in different colors, rather than ordinary stationers' carbon paper.

To transfer the design, place the fabric on a flat surface with strips of masking tape at the corners. If the fabric is too large to be stuck to the surface, pin the relevant portion in place with drawing pins. Make a tracing of the design and tape this over the fabric, then slip the carbon paper face down between the fabric and the tracing and trace over the design outlines.

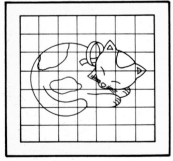

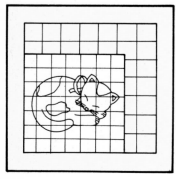

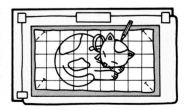

QUILTING

Quilting is a way of holding three layers – top, padding and backing fabric – together and at the same time adding to the decorative effect. Most of the quilted projects in this book, such as the children's sleeping bags, can be worked either by hand or by machine.

If you have never quilted before, make some small experimental samples first to see which method you prefer. You may find that the thickest padding will not pass easily through your sewing machine and is equally hard to stitch by hand, in which case use a thinner one.

Hand quilting equipment

Traditionally, hand quilting was worked with the three layers stretched out on a frame, but unless you already have a frame, it is generally better to buy a quilting hoop, which is cheaper and much less bulky. This is much like an embroidery hoop, only larger, and is either supported on its own stand or rested against the edge of the table, leaving both hands free for quilting.

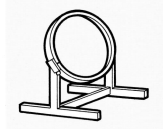

You can either use ordinary thread appropriate to the fabric or special quilting thread, which is heavier and stronger. It is useful to have a block of beeswax, available from large stores, through which you can run the threads to prevent them from twisting during sewing.

Use short fine needles – No. 8 or 9 betweens – and a thimble.

Hand sewing

Before sewing, tack the layers together thoroughly. Tack from the center out to the corners and to equally spaced points at the edges, then start again at the center and tack in concentric squares spaced about 6in (15cm) apart. To avoid ending up with a concentration of tacking knots at the center of the work, take a thread long enough to run from corner to corner. Start at the center, leaving a long tail of thread, and tack out to one corner; return to the center and rethread the needle, then tack out to the opposite corner.

To position the work in a hoop, place the central part of the tacked work over the inside ring. Smooth over the outer edges and slide the outer ring in place. Then tighten the adjustment screw to hold the materials taut. After quilting, remove and reposition over the next section.

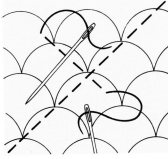

Quilt from the centre of the work outwards, holding the work in the hoop to keep the layers evenly stretched. Take a fairly short length of thread, about 16in (40cm) and knot one end. Lose the knot in between the top and bottom layers and quilt with a small, even running stitch. It helps to wear a thimble on the index finger of your sewing hand. Keep the other hand under the work to guide the needle back up again after it has passed through all three layers.

Complete one section before moving on and never leave the work in a hoop overnight. To fasten off, tie a knot close to the last stitch, take the thread to the back, losing the knot in the padding. Run the needle along the padding, bring it back up to the top and cut the end.

Machine quilting

For machine quilting, use a slightly longer stitch than normal and loosen off the tension a little. Do not begin or end with a back stitch – the ends should be pulled through to the back, knotted in pairs and pulled up into the padding with a needle.

Stitch from the center to the edge, where possible, working out to one edge then returning to the center and working out to the other edge. Hold the work flat with your hands, but avoid pushing the layers apart.

A quilting foot is a useful attachment which enables you to make evenly spaced lines of quilting, but it is not essential because you can always mark the lines on the fabric instead.

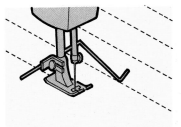

PATCHWORK

Choosing fabrics

As with appliqué, the easiest fabric to use is pure dress-weight cotton, but you can also use silks or wools. Avoid mixing fabrics of different weights and types as they will tend to pull unevenly against each other. The exception to the rule is those patchworks which are applied to a background fabric, like the Crazy Cover (pp62-5), where it is perfectly possible to mix fabrics and textures.

Making templates

The simplest way is to draw each shape to the full size on graph paper, adhere the paper to card and then cut it out with a craft knife.

For hand sewing, make templates to the full size minus seam allowances. For machine sewing, make templates to include seam allowances.

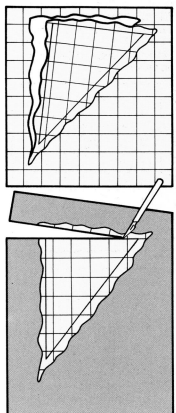

Marking and cutting

For hand-sewn work, start by drawing a guideline on the wrong side of the fabric, parallel to the selvedge and at least a seam allowance away from it. Place the template against this line, starting at one corner of the piece, and draw around it. Add a seam allowance. Position the template on the line again, a seam allowance away from the outer marked line (cutting edge of first patch), and repeat. As you work, try to align the patches against each other as much as possible to save fabric.

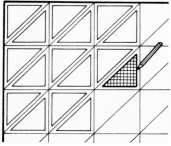

Cut the patches out along the outer marked line – the inner line is the sewing line – and sort them into piles according to shape and color.

For machine patchwork, you only need the cutting edge to be marked, since the edge of the presser foot or a piece of masking tape stuck to the throat plate can be used as a guide to the seamline.

For both hand and machine work, try to mark out patches so that as many edges as possible are in alignment with the grain lines of the fabric.

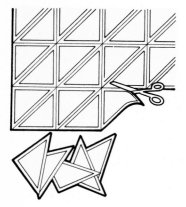

Hand sewing

Pin two patches with right sides together, putting a pin at each corner first and then at intervals along the sewing line. Insert the pins at right angles to the sewing line. Take a length of thread about 14in (35cm) long and thread your needle. Make a knot in the other end, which should be the end you have just cut. Using a small, neat running stitch, sew the patches together, sewing along the marked seamline only, not in the seam allowance. Finish with two or three back stitches and press the seam to one side. Join patches into rows and then rows into larger sections, always pressing seams to one side.

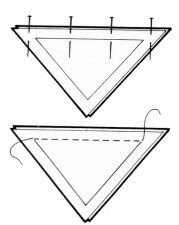

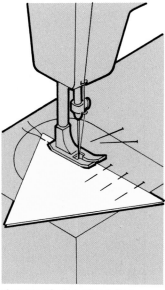

Machine sewing

Pin patches together, pinning across the unmarked seamline. Set your machine to 12 stitches per inch (about 5 per centimeter) and stitch patches together, removing pins before they pass under the presser foot. You can

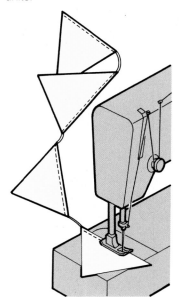

join several pairs of patches together at one time, leaving a short length of thread between each pair. When you have finished, separate the pairs and press all seams open, before joining the patches into larger units.

APPLIQUE

Choosing fabrics

A wide range of fabrics can be used for appliqué, but some are easier to sew than others or are preferable because they are easier to clean. Although you can use old clothes and rummage findings, be sure that the fabric is still in good condition and has plenty of wear left in it.

Because appliqué fabrics are sewn to a background, you can mix different weights and types of fabric in the same work, but for beginners, the easiest fabric to use is pure dress-weight cotton. Synthetic fibres or polyester/cotton blends can be used but they tend to be springy, which makes them more difficult to shape and sew.

For the background, choose a firm fabric such as a good-quality cotton, which will wear well. Do not, however, choose one that is so firm that it creates sewing problems.

Making templates

You will need a template for each separate piece to be applied. Start by making a full-scale drawing of the design, then make a tracing of this, numbering each individual piece.

Take a second sheet of tracing paper and make a tracing of each numbered piece and then cut these tracings out. You can either use them as templates or adhere them to thin card, which will give you a firmer edge.

Marking and cutting

Place the template right side up on the right side of the chosen fabric. Mark round the edge with a well-sharpened pencil in a color close to that of the fabric. The applied pieces will be easier to sew and will blend in with the background more smoothly if you try to cut them so that the grainlines of the pieces lie in the same direction as the grainlines of the background fabric, so use your design drawing as a reference when marking.

Pieces that are machine sewn should be cut out without seam allowances. For hand-sewn pieces, leave a ¼in (6mm) seam allowance all around when cutting out. Very faintly pencil the number of the piece on the back of the patch.

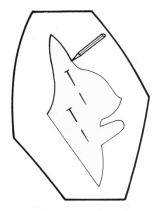

Preparing and positioning

Machine-sewn pieces are pinned and tacked directly to the fabric. Hand-sewn pieces must first be prepared by turning under and tacking the seam allowances (if one piece overlaps another, the portion which will lie underneath need not be turned and tacked).

It may help you to achieve a good line if you first staystitch around the piece, stitching within the seam allowance and close to the inner line, either by machine or by hand, using a small running stitch.

On convex curves, as on a sun shape, it is a good idea to run a gathering thread around the curve. Take small stitches, keeping within the seam allowance, but starting with a knot on the right side of the fabric so that the thread can easily be removed. Take notches out of the seam allowance at regular intervals to remove fullness.

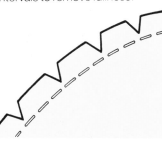

On concave curves, clip halfway to the seamline at regular intervals, using sharp embroidery scissors.

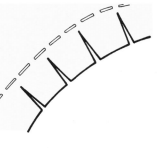

Cut across tops of points, within seam allowance, and turn them under. Turn down cut point first, then fold in the two sides.

Tack with small tacking stitches, pressing the edge firmly with your fingers as you tack.

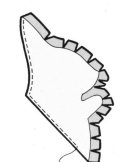

When all the pieces are prepared, position them on the fabric, using your design tracing as a guide. Pin and then tack the pieces, stitching about ⅛in (4mm) from the edge.

Hand sewing

Sew the pieces to the background with tiny blind stitches, beginning with a knot hidden in the seam allowance and ending with one between the applied piece and the backing fabric. Use thread that closely matches the appliqué fabric.

If applied pieces overlap each other, cut the underlying pieces to allow for about ¼in (6mm) overlap. Prepare the fabric pieces as usual, but do not turn under any edges that will be subsequently covered. Pin and tack the underlying pieces in position first and then the overlying ones, making sure that all raw edges are covered. When you come to sew the pieces, make sure that your stitches pass through both the layers of appliqué and the background.

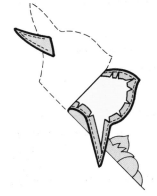

Machine appliqué

Make sure that your machine is in good working order and that you have the appropriate threads for the fabric. You should also check that you have a good supply of the right needles for the fabric or fabrics and that they are new and sharp.

Position the pieces as for hand-sewn work and tack them. Set your machine to a close zigzag stitch and machine round the edge of each shape. To avoid puckers, try to work from the central point of each shape outwards or, if one end of a piece lies under another, work in toward that end so that excess fabric can be tucked under the overlying piece. On curves, raise and lower the presser foot in order to achieve a smooth line.

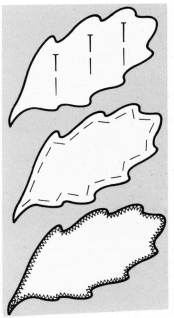

If you set your machine to too close a stitch you may find that it clogs up. In this case, use a more open zigzag and, if necessary, go round the stitches a second time.

You can start and finish with backstitching or, if this is difficult, just pull the threads through to the back and fasten them. When you have finished stitching, remove any tacking stitches that still show and trim away any raw edges or loose threads with sharp embroidery scissors.

SUNSHINE AND SHADOW

Two simple but elegant design ideas for quick, stylish curtains, using nothing more complicated than squares. The plastic curtain with its square appliquéd pockets containing black and white or multicoloured strands of cotton will hide a dull view but let the sunshine flood into your room. The shadow-design curtains are made from pure white cotton scattered with gray squares stitched on top of black sateen ones, slightly staggered to give the shadow effect. They are made in three panels to allow the air to circulate and to create the perfect cool, calm setting for a holiday home.

MATERIALS

SUNSHINE CURTAIN
Shower curtaining
Transparent plastic for the squares
Shiny mercerized cotton in a variety of colors
Adhesive tape
Sewing thread in a variety of colors

SHADOW CURTAINS
Plain white cotton fabric for curtains
Scrap of black sateen
Scrap of gray flannelette
Matching threads

DIRECTIONS

SUNSHINE CURTAIN
▦ Make up the curtain to the desired size, with double ⅜in (1cm) side hems and a double 1½in (4cm) base hem. At the top, either make a cased heading or attach a fine heading tape.
▦ For the border, cut out 3in (7cm) squares of plastic and for the central motifs, 3½in (9cm) squares.
▦ Position each square in turn on the curtain and hold in place with small amounts of adhesive tape. Zigzag stitch three sides, using two contrasting threads, one for the top and one in the bobbin. Insert strands of mercerized cotton and close the remaining side of each square.

SHADOW CURTAIN
▦ Make up three curtain panels to the correct size, with double ⅜in (1cm) side hems and a double 1½in (4cm) base hem. At the top, either make a cased heading or attach a fine heading tape.
▦ Decide on the size of the appliqué squares: 4in (10cm) is a good size. Make a template from thin card and mark out a sufficient number of squares on the gray and black fabrics. For each square, use the template to mark the foldline on the wrong side of the fabric, then add a ¼in (6cm) seam allowance all around.
▦ Cut out each square along the outer marked line and turn the seam allowance to the wrong side, cutting across each corner point and mitering the corners to reduce bulk. Pin and tack all around each square.
▦ Position the black squares on each curtain and tack them vertically in place. Set your machine to a medium-length stitch and, with matching thread, stitch around the outer edge of each square.
▦ Remove the tacking stitches, then position a gray square to overlap each black one and repeat the process, again using matching thread.
▦ When all the stitching is complete, remove the remaining tacking stitches and pull the ends through to the wrong side. Fasten them through the stitching at the back or, alternatively, knot them in pairs and cut off the ends.

simple squares for instant style

SYMPHONY IN NEUTRALS

The subtly varied shapes of this small cloth, emphasized by a restrained use of textured neutrals, are derived from the fabrics used for *furoshiki*, the square cloths in which the Japanese traditionally wrap gifts. Like so many other aspects of Japanese life, *furoshiki* are an art form in themselves, and this small cloth could be used either as a wall hanging or to grace the center of a small occasional table.

MATERIALS

28in (70cm) square of fine white linen for the base fabric
⅞yd (80cm) of 36in (90cm) wide ecru raw silk for the border and appliqué

Scraps of black and white linens for the appliqué
Matching threads

DIRECTIONS

▦ Scale up the patterns for the motifs and cut out the shapes from thin card or tracing paper.

▦ Mark each pattern out on the right side of the appropriate fabric and add a ¼in (6mm) allowance all around. Cut out beyond the seam allowance and then

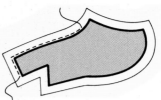

staystitch around each motif, stitching within the seam allowance and just outside the marked foldline. Cut out each motif along the outer line.

▦ Fold the seam allowance to the wrong side all around each piece, pinning and then tacking. To form smooth curves, take notches out of the seam allowance on outward-facing curves and make clips up to the foldline on inward-facing curves.

▦ When the shapes are prepared, pin them to the background, as shown, and tack them vertically in place. Where shapes overlap each other, pin,

tack and stitch the bottom layer first, and then apply the next layer on top of the first. Use matching thread to sew each piece in place with small, neat slipstitches.

▦ When the appliqué is finished, remove tacking stitches. Take the remaining ecru silk and cut four border strips 4in (10cm) deep, cutting across the full 36in (90cm) width of the fabric.

▦ Taking a ⅜in (1cm) seam, attach two side strips, stopping ⅜in (1cm) short of the edge at each corner. Next attach the top and bottom strips in the same way, so that they meet exactly at the corners of the appliquéd piece and the ends are left free. Fold the ends of the side strips diagonally under to make mitered corners and sew them down by hand. Neaten.

▦ Trim across the corners and finish the border with a ⅜in (1cm) double hem.

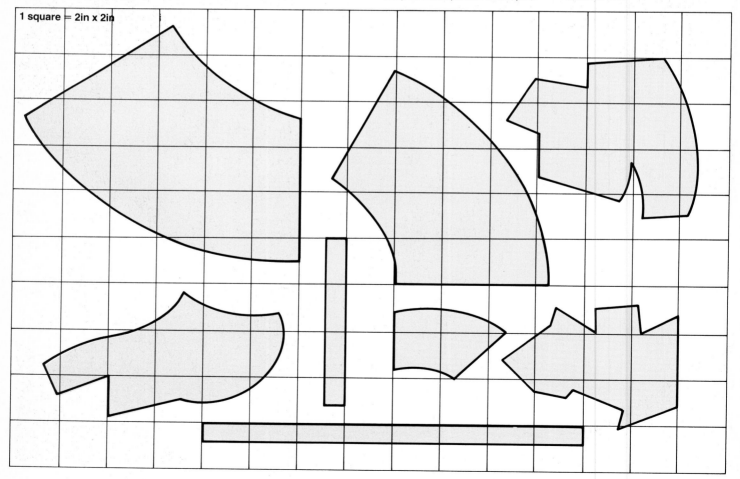

1 square = 2in x 2in

Japanese-style geometrics

CUBIST THROW

If your friends think that appliqué is all pretty little pictures of birds and flowers, startle them with this restrained but beautiful sofa throw based on a picture by Braque. The muted shades overlap against a plain background, and the clearly defined borders give the effect of a picture frame. Although we suggest how to make the borders, the size, coloring and placement of the patches is up to you – this is your own work of art.

Finished size: approximately 51in (130cm) square

MATERIALS

48in (120cm) wide brushed cotton as follows:	⅝yd (50cm) beige
1⅓yd (1.2m) cream	Scraps of brown, beige, rust and
1¼yd (1m) brown	gray plain and patterned
¾yd (70cm) dark brown	brushed cotton fabrics
	Matching threads

DIRECTIONS

◫ Cut out one 37½in (96cm) square of brown fabric and center it on the cream square. Pin, tack and zigzag stitch in place.
◫ From beige fabric, cut four strips, each 44in × 2½in (111cm × 6cm). Mark two lines by tacking all around the cream square 2in (4.5cm) and 4½in (10.5cm) from the outer edge, making sure that the stitching is parallel with the edge.
◫ Tack the first beige strip in place between the tacked lines. Lay the next strip with right sides together over the first strip. At the corner, stitch through all layers of fabric on the diagonal from inner to outer corner. Bring the second strip down to right side and tack along second side.
◫ Work each corner in the same way, until the last corner: turn under the last end on the diagonal and crease. Place over the first end and stitch together along creased line. Zigzag stitch all the strips in place along both edges.
◫ Cut out rectangles of rust and beige fabrics each 2½in × 1¼in (6cm × 3cm) and alternate them along the outer edge of the beige border, leaving spaces the same size in between. Pin, tack and zigzag in position.
◫ From a variety of plain and patterned fabrics cut out squares

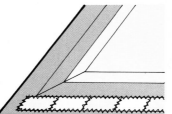

of assorted sizes, from about 12in (30cm) to 6in (15cm). Lay the squares in a haphazard fashion over the central brown square, sometimes overlapping. Pin and zigzag stitch each layer in place.
◫ For the outer edges, cut four strips of dark brown fabric each 50½in × 5½in (127cm × 13cm). Fold each strip in half lengthways. At the ends, bring up raw edges to fold, producing a mitered effect, and press. Cut along creased line. Unfold. Pin, tack and stitch short edges of strips together, along

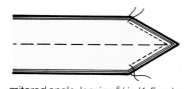

mitered angle, leaving ⅝in (1.5cm) unstitched at outer edges. Press seam open at each corner, making a miter. Turn under ⅝in (1.5cm) all around inner edges; slide mitered border over the edge of the work to meet the oblong strip border. Topstitch.

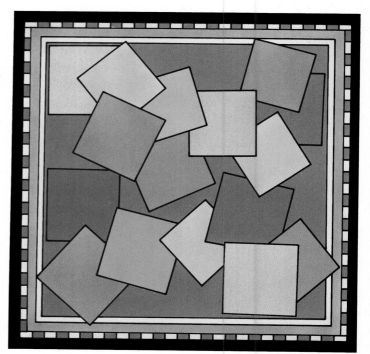

an appliqué picture with a difference

WINDOW CHIC

The different sheens and textures of this complex appliqué shade provide interest and variety while allowing ample daylight to filter through in a subtle range of nuances and tones. Made with a combination of machine appliqué and embroidery, together with cutwork, it is not the sort of thing which a complete beginner can run up in an evening, but if you have a certain degree of skill and confidence, the result will be very rewarding, and very chic.

Finished size: 24in (60cm) wide × 36in (90cm) long

MATERIALS

1¼yd (1.1m) each of 48in (122cm) wide white sateen and white cotton net
⅝yd (50cm) square of white satin
Matching thread

Shiny white machine embroidery thread
Length of dowel or curtain pole, plus hanging hooks, or a roller blind kit

DIRECTIONS

▦ Fix hooks on either side of window to hold pole.

▦ From sateen, cut one piece 43in × 24½in (110cm × 62cm). Cut a piece of cotton net the same size and place the two with right sides together and pin and tack down one (long) side. Machine, taking ⅜in (1cm) allowance. Repeat for other side, this time pulling net over to overlap raw edge of sateen by ¼in (6mm).

▦ Turn right side out and press side hems. Working across and vertically, tack the fabrics together at 4in (10cm) intervals.

▦ Scale up the three appliqué motifs from the diagram and cut the appropriate numbers from white satin. Take a long rule and a sharp, light-colored pencil and lightly draw in the vertical and horizontal lines, using the diagram as a guide and starting 10in (25cm) up from the base edge.

▦ Pin and tack the motifs in position then, using a close zigzag stitch, carefully stitch around each piece. With the same stitch, complete the remaining lines of the design, stitching up to the top edge of the blind. After stitching, pull all loose threads to the wrong side and fasten off.

▦ Using sharp-pointed scissors, carefully cut out the sateen only from areas indicated on the diagram, to reveal the net.

▦ At the base, turn up ⅜in (1cm) and then 1½in (4cm) to form a hem.

▦ Turn ⅜in (1cm) then 5in (12cm) to wrong side at top of blind, to form a casing. Pin, tack and stitch across. Insert dowel/pole and hang on hooks at either side of window.

ROLLER BLIND

▦ Position brackets on each side of the window with pin hole on the right and square bracket on the left. Trim roller to fit – hammer on end cap with pin.

▦ Turn down top edge for ⅝in (1.5cm) to right side. Lay roller across blind top; with folded edge to marked edge on roller; hammer tacks in place along folded edge.

▦At the base turn up ⅜in (1cm) and then 1½in (4cm) to form a casing; pin, tack and stitch one end and across the casing. Trim lath to ⅝in (1.5cm) shorter than the casing. Slide wood into casing; slipstitch open end to close. Make up a cord pull and fasten cord holder centrally to wrong side of casing.

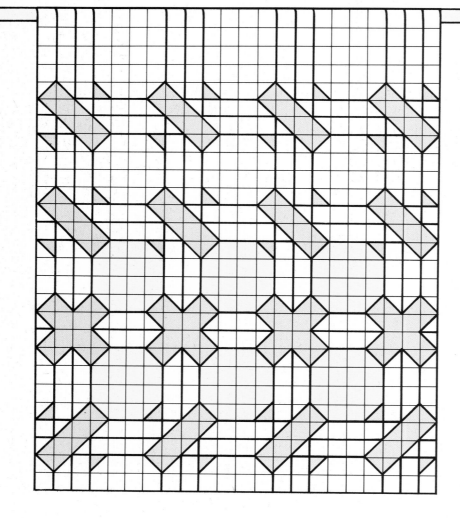

1 square = 1in x 1in

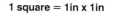 satin applique motifs

sateen cutouts

——— zigzag stitching lines

the sophisticated elegance of white-on-white

CAT AND MOUSE GAME

Can Miss Mouse find her way through the maze and arrive safely at the birthday party without falling into Mistress Cat's claws, or will her human friend have to help her? This enchanting duvet, with its appliquéd cat and maze and embroidered mice, will keep a little child happily absorbed for ages. The size given would fit a crib, but you could easily enlarge the design and work it on a bigger cover.

Finished size: 147in × 39in (20cm × 100cm)

MATERIALS

1½yd (1.3m) of 90in (228cm) wide straw-colored sheeting ¾in (2cm) wide cotton tape: ¾yd (70cm) of dark blue, 2¼yd (2m) of medium blue, 3½yd (3m) of pale blue, 2¼yd (2m) of pale green, 1¾yd (1.6m) of medium green, 1⅓yd (1.2m) of pale pink, 1yd (1m) of medium pink, 28in (70cm) of dark pink and scrap of gold DMC cotton mouline special in	white, black, gray 415, pink 602, pink 603, pink 604, pink 605, pink 818, brown 434, green 910, green 369 and yellow 743 Velcro spots Scrap of plain white cotton fabric Dressmakers' carbon paper Tracing paper Matching threads

DIRECTIONS

◫ Cut out two pieces of sheeting, each measuring 50in × 40½in (126.5cm × 103cm). Fold a double 1in (2.5cm) wide hem along base edge of each piece, then pin, tack and stitch.

◫ Mark the center both ways on top cover piece. Following the diagram for colors, position lengths of tape around the center point. Pin and tack in place, mitering the corners, to make the first square 6½in × 6½in (16cm × 16cm). The remaining squares are successively 1¼in (3cm) further out. Where tapes meet and at ends, tuck under raw edges for ¼in (6mm) to finish.

◫ When all the tape is in position, topstitch in place, close to edges on both sides of the tape.

◫ Trace off the cat motif and mark it on the white cotton. Cut out, leaving ⅝in (1.5cm) allowance all around. On the outward-facing (convex) curves, make a line of small running stitches, leaving the ends free and sewing just outside the marked line.

◫ Trim seam allowance down to ¼in (6mm) then turn it under and tack all around, pulling up the gathering thread slightly and taking out notches, so that the curve lies smooth. Pin the cat in position on cover and tack it in place around the edge, just in from the fold, then stitch it in place with small, neat slipstitches. Using

catch-me-if-you-can cover

three strands of DMC thread, outline the areas to be embroidered with chainstitch, then fill in with long and short stitch.

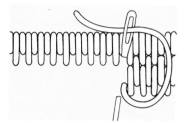

▦ Trace off the mice and table motifs and, using dressmakers' carbon paper, mark them on cover as shown in diagram. Using three strands of DMC thread, embroider, following the diagram for colors.

▦ Place the top and bottom cover pieces with right sides together, stitch alongside base hem, leaving a central opening of 24in (60cm).

▦ Place the pieces with wrong sides together and stitch round top and side edges, ⅝in (1cm) in from edge. Trim close to seamline; turn wrong side out and press, then stitch again, ¼in (6mm) from fold, enclosing first seam.

▦ Turn cover right side out and stitch Velcro spots, spacing them equally on both sides of opening.

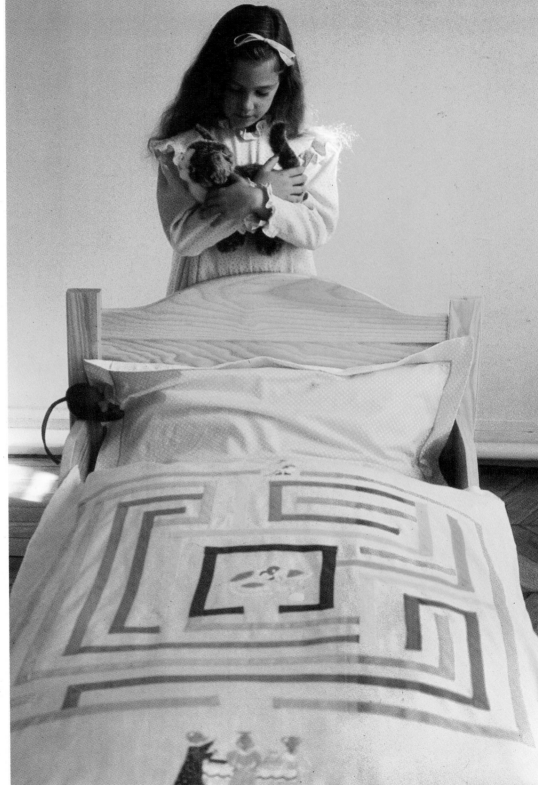

KEY
A White
B Black
C Gray 415
D Pink 602
E Pink 603
F Pink 604
G Pink 605
H Pink 818
I Brown 434
J Green 910
K Green 369
L Yellow 743

FRIENDLY TIGER

This amiable tiger looks as if he couldn't hurt a fly: use him to transform plain shorts and straps or a pinafore into a fun outfit that will give enormous pleasure to a youngster. The head is very quick and easy to make, and the details can either be embroidered on, as they are here, or if you prefer you could use plain cotton and fabric paints.

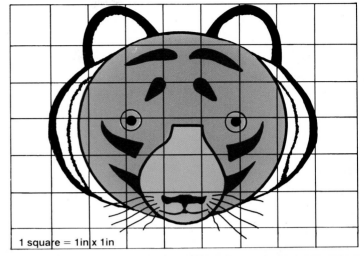

1 square = 1in x 1in

MATERIALS

6½in (16cm) square of black felt
6½in × 5in (16cm × 12cm) of ginger-colored woolen fabric
5½in × 5in (14cm × 12cm) of backing fabric
Small amount of suitable filling,
for muzzle
Black, white and green embroidery cottons
Strong black thread for whiskers
Dressmakers' pattern paper
Matching threads

DIRECTIONS

▦ Draw up patterns from diagram and cut out as stated.
▦ Embroider features on face using black embroidery cotton. Embroider nose and mouth on muzzle. Position muzzle on face; tuck under raw edge; pin and stitch in place adding a small amount of filling as you work. Thread black thread through muzzle and knot at each side for whiskers.

▦ Place face on head, tuck under raw edge; pin and stitch in place. Embroider white stripes on each side of the head.
▦ Place inner ears centrally on two outer ears. Pin and stitch in place. Place ears in pairs with plain ears with right sides together; pin and stitch all around, leaving base edges open. Trim and turn to right side. Place ears to head front at marked positions.
▦ Place heads with right sides together; pin and stitch together all around, catching in ears and leaving an opening at base. Trim and turn to right side. Turn in opening edges in line with remainder of the seam and slipstitch together to close.
▦ Position tiger head to straps; pin and stitch in place.

MEXICAN HEATWAVE

In addition to hot sun and even hotter food, Mexico is well known for its bold, eye-catching art, alive with colorful flowers, brilliant birds and strange, fierce gods. These cushion covers, inspired by elaborate Mexican paper cut-outs, are guaranteed to bring you a touch of Latin American sunshine even in the depths of winter.

Size: to fit cushion pads measuring 16in × 12in (40cm × 30cm)

MATERIALS

For each cover:	Dressmakers' pattern paper
⅝yd (50cm) of 36in (90cm) wide white linen	Marking pen
	12in (30cm) zipper
18in × 14in (45cm × 35cm) of felt in pink, yellow or blue	Matching threads
	Masking tape

DIRECTIONS

▦ For cushion front, cut out a piece of linen 17¼in × 13¼in (43cm × 33cm).

▦ Scale up the chosen design on dressmakers' pattern paper then carefully cut out the shaded area from the diagram. You can do this with good paper scissors, but it will be easier to cut accurately if you tape the design down to a good cutting surface, to hold it steady, and use a craft knife.

▦ Place the pattern centrally on the felt and tape the corners to hold it steady, then tape the edges of the felt to your worktop. Carefully mark out the design using a marking pen.

▦ Using a pair of sharp-pointed scissors, cut out the design.

▦ Center the felt on the cushion front. Pin and tack it in place, taking care not to stretch it. Using matching thread, neatly slipstitch around all the cut-out sections and the edge.

▦ For the cushion back, cut a piece of fabric 17¼in × 14½in (43cm × 36cm). Cut in half lengthways across the center. With right sides together and taking a ⅝in (1.5cm) seam allowance, pin, tack and stitch 2½in (6.5cm) in from either side. Tack remainder of seam and position zipper centrally behind the tacked section. Pin, tack and stitch zip in place. Open zipper.

▦ Place cushion front to cushion back, right sides together. Pin, tack and stitch together all around, just beyond outer edge of felt. Trim and finish seam. Turn to right side through zipper. Insert cushion pad and close zipper.

▦ Repeat this method to make up the remaining cushion covers using the two other colors of felt.

CUT-OUT DESIGN

If the designs given here are not suited to your decor, you can easily make your own patterns using the method shown here, which is based on the elaborate style of appliqué known as Hawaiian. The main difference between designs produced by this method and the Mexican patterns given here, is that the Hawaiian method produces symmetrical shapes radiating from a central point, which are placed on a square or circular background.

Take a square piece of paper and fold it in half, making sure that the edges meet exactly.

Take the paper and fold it in half again, once more checking that the corners and edges meet neatly.

Fold the paper again, this time diagonally, folding it so that all the folded edges lie on one short side of the diagonal fold and all the cut edges lie on the other short side.

Draw a design on the folded paper, as shown, making sure that the design is connected along the diagonal and the folded edges on the short (right) side.

Cut out along the outline(s) and then unfold the design. Make several patterns before choosing the most attractive and using it as a paper template to mark your felt.

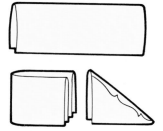

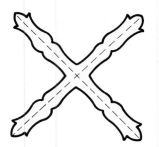

1 square = 4in × 4in

dazzling openwork cushion covers

1 square = 4in x 4in

1 square = 4in x 4in

If you do not want to make a cushion cover, you could use one of these designs to make a bright, attractive wall hanging. Make casings at the top and bottom and insert thin strips of wood or bamboo to hold it flat and provide a hanger.

Sew a felt design to a cloth bag, for an unusual and attractive shoulder bag with an ethnic flavor or, for a more practical and everyday shopping bag, make a vinyl cut-out and glue it in place.

Brighten up the lunch table with appliquéd place mats – the felt will help to protect the table from hot plates.

FOREST TRACK

This table runner, made of matting embellished with an appliquéd satin design of leaves and acorns, would make the perfect accompaniment to an autumnal arrangement of flame- and copper-colored leaves, or dried flowers and seed heads, or to bowls of nuts or russet apples. We have used fusible webbing to adhere the design to the mat ready for sewing, but it could equally well be tacked in place and then trimmed after sewing.

Finished size: 48in × 16in (120cm × 40cm)

MATERIALS

One table runner made of fine matting, 48in × 16in (120cm × 40cm) – if you cannot find a mat of the correct size or fine enough to take the embroidery, use burlap, with the long sides hemmed
Piece of khaki green sateen

20cm × 90cm (8in × 36in) Coats machine embroidery thread in brown, yellow and two greens
One skein of DMC special in 307
Dressmakers' carbon paper
Dressmakers' pattern paper
Fusible webbing

METHOD

▦ Draw up the design from the diagram. Mark the design on one side of the fusible webbing. Cut out outside the outline. Fuse on to the wrong side of sateen fabric. Carefully cut out around the marked outline.
▦ Remove backing and position along one short edge of runner, as shown in diagram and picture, and pin in place. Press in position. Remove pins and press in place again, this time over a damp cloth.

▦ Test the zigzag stitch on the machine and select the best length and width. Using threads as shown in the diagram, carefully stitch round each leaf. Embroider inside the acorns again, by hand, in satin stitch.
▦ Using sharp-pointed scissors, carefully cut out enclosed portions and along the outlines of the leaves overlapping the edge of the runner.
▦ Repeat to decorate the opposite end of the runner in the same way.

1 square = 2in x 2in

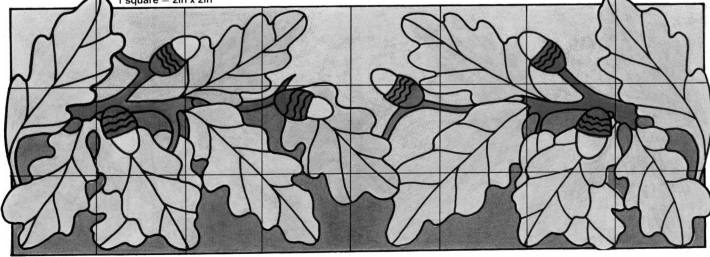

KAZAK QUILT

These felt picture symbols were taken from a book on the folk art of the Kazaks, a nomadic tribe of central Asia. This quilt, made from two layers of flannel with a thick layer of padding in between, would be ideal for keeping at bay the sub-zero temperatures of a Kazak winter. The symbols are drawn and cut with precision and machined on to the top before the quilt is assembled and edged with black and green sheeting.

Finished size: 48in × 60in (120cm × 156cm)

MATERIALS

3½yd (3.2m) of 48in (120cm) wide gray flannel	heavy-weight padding
⅝yd (50cm) of 70in (178cm) wide green sheeting	Small amounts of red, turquoise, blue, prune, pink and saffron yellow felt, for motifs
½yd (40cm) of 70in (178cm) wide black sheeting	Suitable filling to pad motifs
2¾yd (2.4m) of 36in (90cm) wide	Dressmakers' pattern paper
	Matching threads

DIRECTIONS

▨ From gray flannel cut two pieces each 60in × 39in (156cm × 100cm).

▨ Draw up the motif designs from the diagram and, following the diagram for colors, carefully cut out from felts. Pin the motifs carefully on one flannel piece, as shown in the picture and diagram. Using matching thread, carefully tack each motif in place, sewing close to the edge and taking small stitches. Stuff a small amount of filling inside each motif as you stitch.

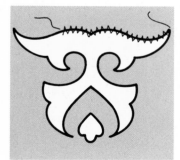

▨ Set the sewing machine to a close zigzag stitch – test on a spare piece of fabric before stitching. Zigzag stitch all around each motif. After stitching, take all the loose threads to the wrong side and tie in pairs.

▨ From green sheeting cut out one piece 61½in × 17in (160cm × 43cm). Taking a ⅝in (1.5cm) seam allowance and with right sides together, pin, tack and stitch one long edge of green sheeting to one long edge of front quilt piece, overlapping the flannel by ¾in (2cm) at either end. Repeat, to stitch remaining long edge of sheeting to one edge of quilt back in the same way. Fold the pieces together, forming a 8in (20cm) wide band of green sheeting at one edge.

▨ Cut two pieces of padding each 48in (120cm) long. Align the long edges against each other and join them together with herringbone stitch. Turn over and herringbone stitch on the other side to link them closely and securely. Trim padding to measure 48in × 60in (120cm × 156cm).

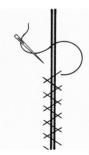

keeping warm on the Mongolian steppes

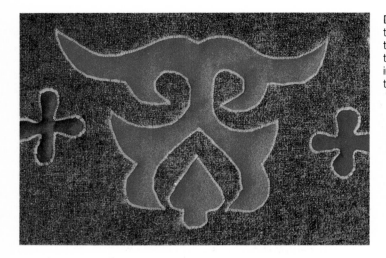

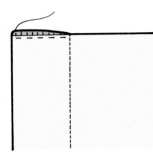

▦ Sandwich the padding inside the quilt front and back; pin, and tack all the layers together. Fold the raw ends of the sheeting strip in to meet each other and cover the padding. Slipstitch to close.

▦ Cut three strips of black sheeting: two 3in × 40½in (8cm × 101.5cm) and one 3in × 61½in (8cm × 160cm). Turn in the long edges on all strips by ⅝in (1.5cm) and press. Fold all strips down the center and press.

▦ Take the two shorter strips and fold in ⅝in (1.5cm) at either short end and press, then position to cover raw ends on two short sides of quilt. Topstitch in place with white zigzag stitching. Where black strip meets green slipstitch in black to close.

▦ Apply final black strip in the same way, folding the raw ends into a miter and slipstitching.

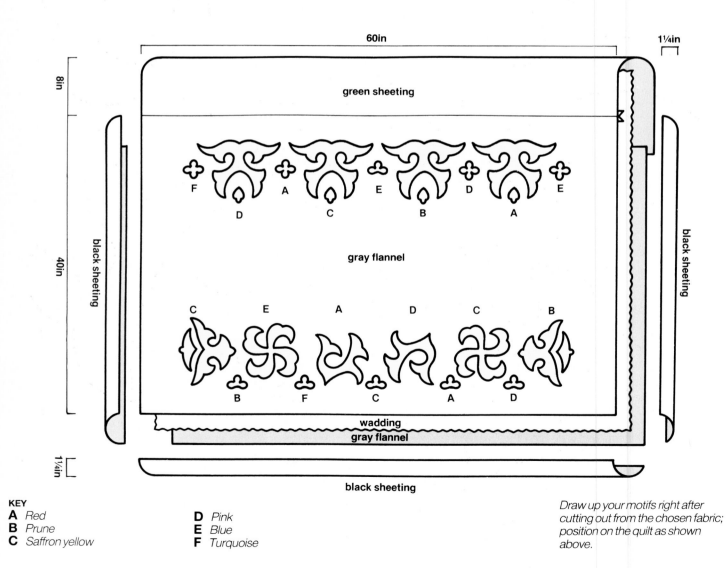

KEY
A *Red*
B *Prune*
C *Saffron yellow*
D *Pink*
E *Blue*
F *Turquoise*

Draw up your motifs right after cutting out from the chosen fabric; position on the quilt as shown above.

1 square = 2in x 2in

fold line

fold line

fold line

fold line

HOARDING SQUIRRELS

Pockets make an ideal hiding place for a winter store cupboard, but will these fluffy scatterbrains be able to remember which pocket is whose? Certainly no child will be able to resist these appliquéd and embroidered squirrels: apply them either to home-made overalls or a pinafore, or to store-bought clothes, adding patch pockets if necessary.

MATERIALS

Scraps of dark brown and printed fabrics	gray 413, dark brown 801, 434 and 738, and green 732
One skein of DMC embroidery silk in each of the following colors: white, pink 3689,	Tracing paper
	Dressmakers' carbon paper
	Matching threads

DIRECTIONS

▦ Scale up the chosen motifs on to tracing paper and mark on the appliqué fabrics (if you are making the jacketed squirrel, cut out a whole body and put the jacket on top). Add a ¼in (6mm) seam allowance around each motif and cut out, leaving a further ¼in (6mm) beyond the outer line.

▦ Staystitch around each motif, just outside the inner line, then cut along the outer line. Clipping into curves and cutting across at the corners, turn under the allowance all around and tack.

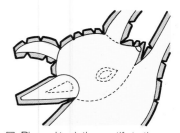

▦ Pin and tack the motifs to the background. Slipstitch each piece in place by hand.

▦ Embroider the remaining details of the animals and nuts, using straight stitch and stem stitch. Halve the embroidery skein when stitching muzzle, eyes, whiskers and claws.

pocket-sized pals for a child

As each squirrel motif is actual size just choose the one you want to use, trace off and mark on to your article of clothing. Squirrels can look just as good on household items as well – hoarding nuts behind a pair of curtains in a child's room or just sitting and eating at the side of a cushion or pillowcase. You do not have to use all the motifs on each piece of work, just pick the one that appeals to you and repeat it at different angles to make up an all-over design.

FRUITY LINEN

An extravagant display of fruit spills out across the sheet and is echoed at the corner of the pillowcases to make a luxurious, exotic and gently crazy set of bed linen. The motifs are embroidered before being appliquéd on to plain sheets – white, peach or yellow would all make good background colors. If you normally use a duvet, buy sheeting and work the appliqué, then make the sheeting into a duvet cover, following the instructions given on pages 18-19.

MATERIALS

Cotton fabric in assorted colors for appliqué	Tracing paper
	Matching threads
Dressmakers' pattern paper	Cotton sheet and pillowcases

DIRECTIONS

▦ Draw up the pattern from the diagrams, carefully aligning the marked edges to give the continuous design. Trace off each motif of the design to form a

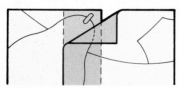

template. Where edges are covered by the next motif, simply straighten the line that will be underneath. Cut out each tracing paper motif.

▦ Pin each template in turn on the right side of the chosen fabric. Mark around the template. Remove the template and cut out, leaving a margin all around of at least ⅜in (1cm).

▦ Position the first motif in place on the sheet, as shown in the picture. Pin and tack in place. In

For each pillowcase, choose a different fruit motif – make up the design separately and then appliqué on to a ready-made pillowcase – a quick and easy way to brighten up a plain set of bed linen.

a dream of plenty

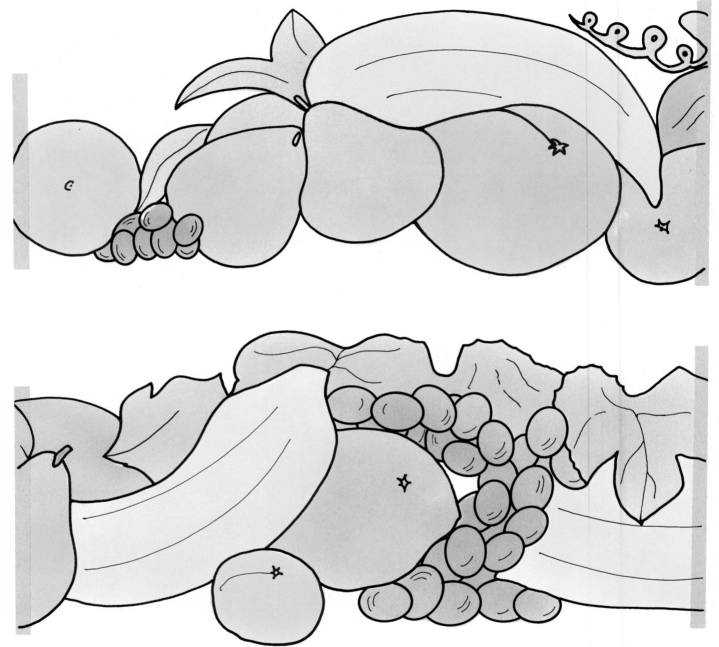

the case of the larger pieces it is advisable to tack vertically across the motif as well as around the outer edge.

▦ With a straight running stitch, stitch in place along the marked outline.

▦ Using a pair of sharp-pointed scissors, trim away excess fabric from the motif, as close to the stitching as possible. Set the

sewing machine to a close zigzag stitch and stitch over the raw edges covering the straight stitching and keeping the stitching even. After stitching, pull all the threads to the wrong side and fasten off securely.

▦ Repeat, to stitch each appliqué in place, overlapping where shown. Add lines of zigzag stitching for ridges and veins.

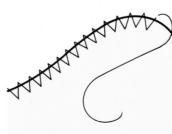

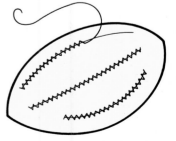

For the pillowcases, trace off one fruit and leaf motif and mark on the appropriate fabrics. Place the motif pieces in position on a piece of backing fabric, using the same fabric as the pillowcase, if possible. Complete by zigzag stitching all around.

Position the motif in one corner of the pillowcase, overlapping the edges. Either stitch in place along the inner line of the zigzag stitch or zigzag stitch in place. Pull the threads to the wrong side and fasten by tying together in pairs.

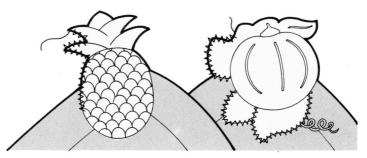

HORSE BAG

No child who has been bitten by the riding bug will want to look this gift horse in the mouth. Although it is designed to amuse, it also serves the practical purpose of holding all the bits and pieces that are needed to groom a pony. Stables are not the cleanest places, so it is made in sturdy, wipe-clean fabric.

MATERIALS

1yd (1m) of 54in (140cm) wide plasticized fabric	Suitable filling
3¼yd (3m) of yellow covered piping cord	1¾yd (1.5m) of thick white cord
¾yd (60cm) of white fringed braid	Eyelets
	Black and white fabric paint
	Dressmakers' pattern paper
	Matching threads

DIRECTIONS

▦ Draw up the patterns for the head, ear and gusset from diagrams, and cut out as stated. For the bag cut one piece 39in × 23in (99cm × 58.5cm) and a 13in (33cm) diameter circle for the bag base.

▦ Make up the ears: working right side up, position covered piping cord along sides of two ear pieces; tack in place. Place the ears right sides together in pairs with remaining plain ears; stitch sides, catching in piping. Trim and turn to right side. Fill each ear and stitch across base. Fold the ears in half matching Fs; stitch from D to E.

▦ Working right side up, position covered piping round front of each head piece from A to C. Place one long edge of gusset to each head piece in turn; pin and stitch in place, leaving opening between As. Trim and turn to right side. Fill head and close opening. Stitch ears to top of head, matching points E to A.

▦ Position a length of fringed braid along one short edge – the back – of bag piece, starting ⅝in (1.5cm) above the bottom edge and finishing 2in (5cm) below the top. Fold bag piece in

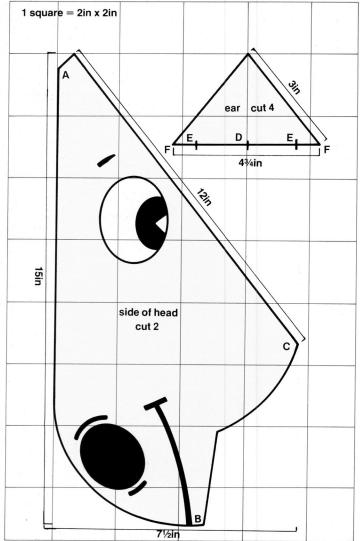

1 square = 2in x 2in

ear cut 4

3in
4¾in
12in
15in
7½in

A
E D E
F F
B
C

side of head cut 2

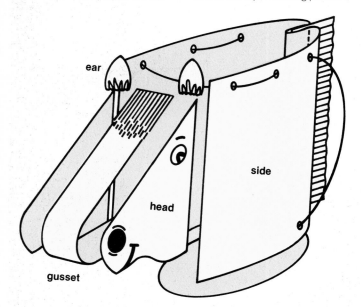

ear

side

head

gusset

half right sides together, matching raw edges; pin and stitch back seam, catching in braid.

▦ Staystitch around bag base, ⅝in (1.5cm) from outer edges. Working right side up, position piping cord around base. Cut a slightly longer length than needed and, at the join, unpick the bias covering and sew the ends together to make a continuous strip; unravel the cord ends and trim strands to different lengths, then twist them together to make a neat joining. Fold covering back over cord.

▦ Snip into allowance up to stitching all around base. Pin and

stitch bag base to base edge of bag piece. Turn down 2in (5cm) along top edge of bag; pin and stitch. Turn bag to right side.

▦ Place horse head on bag at opposite side to back seam, 1¼in (3cm) from bag top; stitch in place by hand. Fold the remaining length of fringing into three and stitch to top of head.

▦ Fix eight eyelets into the top edge of the bag, spacing them about 4¾in (12cm) apart. Fix one eyelet to base of bag, level with back seam. Thread cord through the eyelets and fasten the ends with a knot.

▦ Following diagram, paint in the eyes and nostrils.

practical and fun for pony lovers

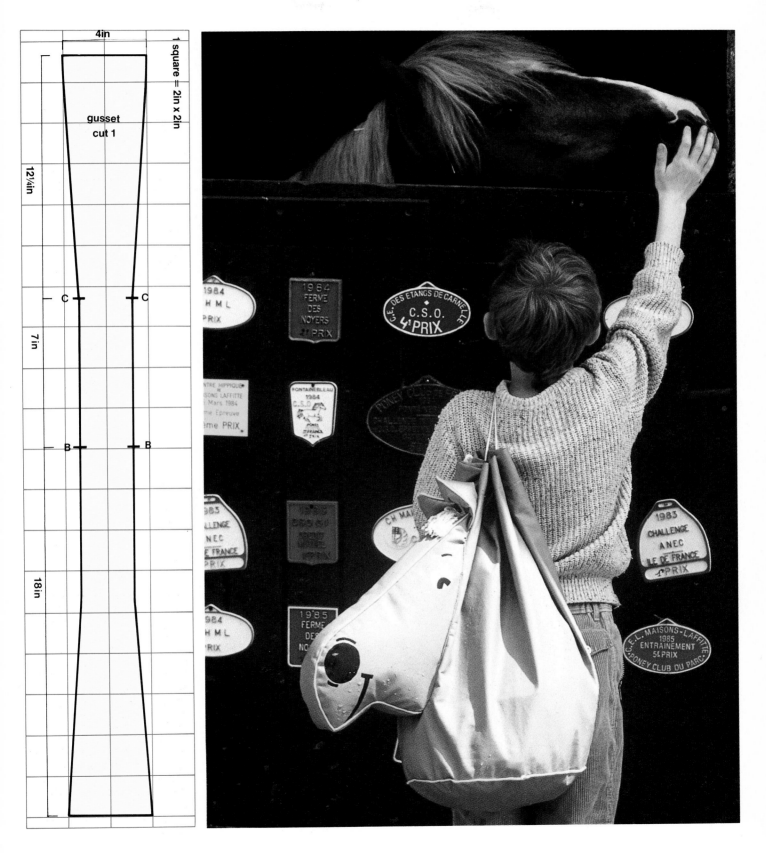

4in

1 square = 2in x 2in

gusset
cut 1

12¼in

C — — C

7in

B — — B

18in

CONVERTIBLE BEDSPREAD

The perfect bedspread for a car enthusiast, and not all that difficult to make. The details are all topstitched to the main body, with a rolled-up sheet added as an optional extra, to make a seat back.

Finished size: 106in × 67in (270cm × 180cm), to fit a 90cm (36in) wide bed – adjust the pattern for a narrower bed

MATERIALS

3yd (2.7m) of 70in (178cm) wide red sheeting
¾yd (60cm) of 36in (90cm) wide dark pink or red sheeting
1yd (1m) 36in (90cm) wide gray/green cotton
2⅛yd (2m) of 36in (90cm) wide black cotton fabric
⅝yd (50cm) of 39in (100cm) wide gray satin
32in × 16in (80cm × 40cm) of

striped cotton or fur fabric
16in × 8in (40cm × 20cm) of yellow cotton fabric
⅝yd (50cm) of 38in (100cm) wide medium-weight polyester padding
Buttons (for dashboard knobs)
1yd (1m) of ¾in (1cm) wide woven black tape and buckles
Dressmakers' pattern paper
Matching threads

DIRECTIONS

⊞ Draw up the patterns of the car from the diagram. From red sheeting, cut out outline, allowing a ⅜in (1cm) allowance all around. Turn the allowance to the wrong side; pin, tack and stitch in place, clipping into curves as necessary.

⊞ Make up the car interior: position the gray/green fabric as shown in the diagram; pin, tack and zigzag stitch in place. Cut out two seats from striped fabric. Repeat, to cut two seats from padding. Place padding then fabric seats in place on the interior; pin, tack and zigzag stitch in place. Topstitch across seats, as shown.

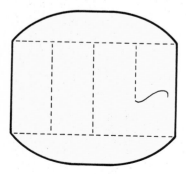

⊞ From gray satin cut two door tops; pin, tack and zigzag stitch in place. Complete the interior with lines of stitching to form the dashboard, adding buttons.

⊞ From black fabric, cut out two steering wheels, adding ⅜in (1cm) allowance all around. Cut one steering wheel from padding, without seam allowance. Clipping into curves, turn under seam allowance around outside and inside of fabric wheels. Place steering wheels with wrong sides together, sandwiching padding in between, and topstitch close to edge, making sure that no padding is visible. Place in position on dashboard and fasten with stitching.

⊞ From dark red or pink fabric, cut four rims to back wheels, as shown in diagram, adding ⅜in (1cm) seam allowance all around. Turn under ¼in (6mm) double hem on two short straight edges of each piece. Edge-finish curves. Cut eight 16in (40cm) diameter wheels from black fabric. With

vroom, vroom, vroooom!

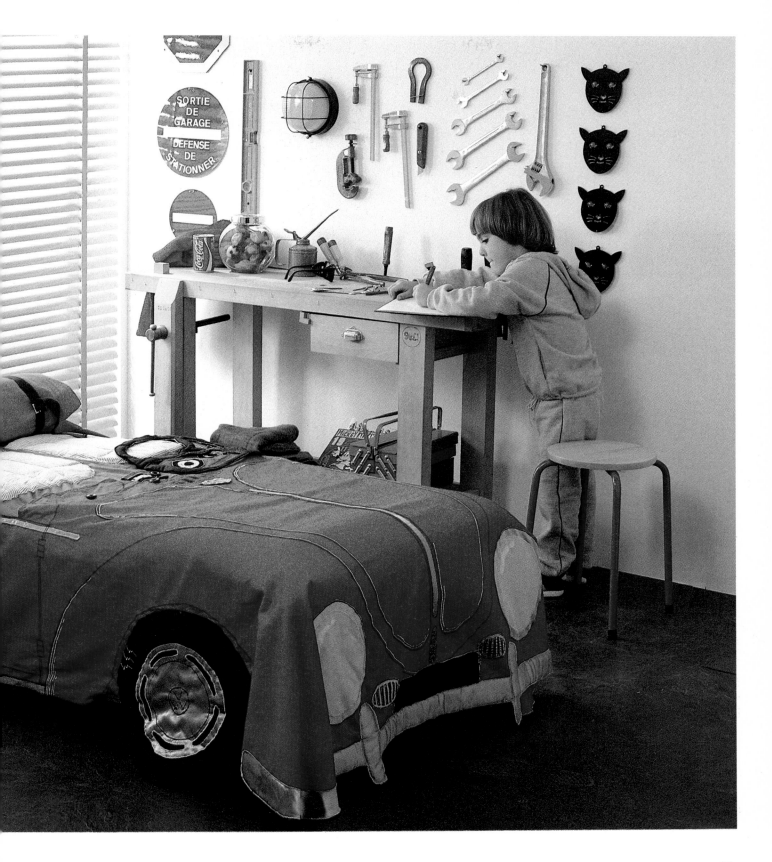

wrong sides together and taking a ¼in (6mm) allowance, stitch wheel

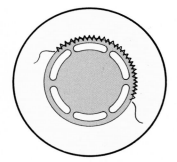

pieces together in pairs, leaving a small opening in each pair. Turn right side out and press. Slipstitch opening in line with seam.

▦ Cut out four hub caps and apply them to the wheels with zigzag stitching, adding center detail. At each wheel position, pin and tack rims to fit behind wheel and edge of main car body. Topstitch in place.

▦ From gray satin cut out two headlights. Cut out two beams from yellow fabric. Place one on top of the other, with right sides up; pin, tack and zigzag stitch in place, adding highlights.

▦ From gray satin cut out bumpers, center hood strip, door sills and handles. Place in position, with bumpers covering outer hemmed edge; pin, tack and zigzag stitch in place. Add number plates, embroidering with the relevant name or number. Complete by zigzag stitching the remaining design lines on the body.

▦ For back straps, make up two 20in (50cm) long straps from tape. Add buckles to one end and cut the opposite end into a point. Position on bedspread, behind the interior, and stitch in place.

There is no need to follow these instructions implicitly; if your child identifies with a different style of car it will be an easy matter to change the position of the lights or alter the bonnet shape. Just move the main parts around till the car resembles one they recognize or just simply change the color.

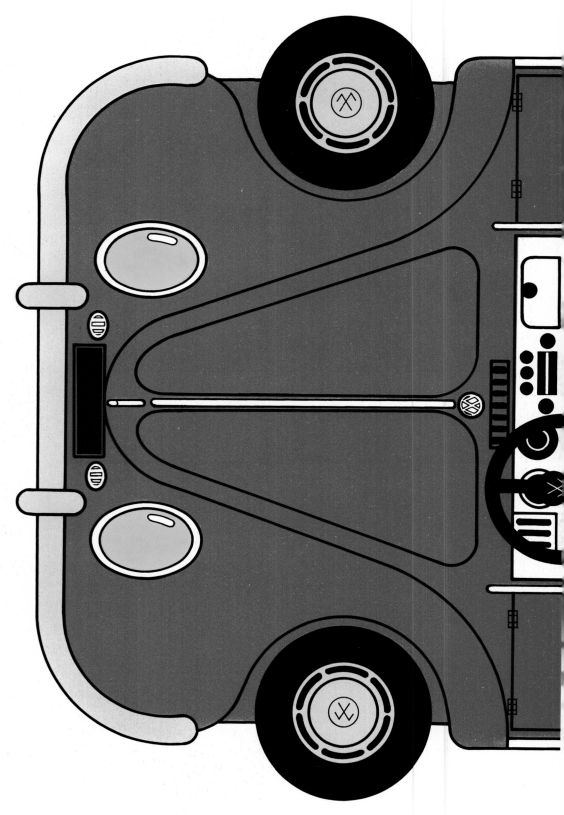

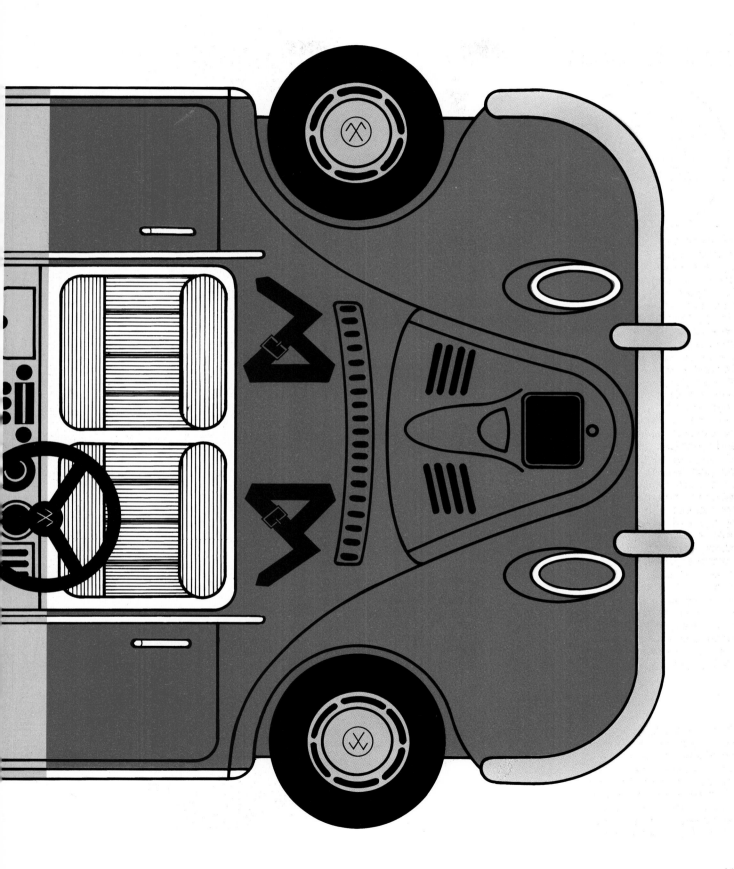

CUSHION MISCELLANY

There is something for everyone in this selection of cushions, which ranges from the realistic fun of the hen and nest to the elegant sophistication of ecru-on-black appliqué or the subtly textured effect of the circular cushion, but all are worked with a machine zigzag stitch. The hen is constructed rather like a tea cosy and is designed to hold bib and wiper, while the nest is securely fastened with ribbons tied spartan fashion. The ecru leaf pattern was inspired by Japanese art and is lightly padded, and the veined pattern of the circular cushion could similarly be worked over a thin layer of padding to give a slight relief effect.

MATERIALS

THE HEN
1yd (1m) of 36in (90cm) wide
  chestnut-colored cotton
  fabric
16in × 32in (40cm × 80cm) of
  medium-weight polyester
  padding

Scraps of felt or cotton in yellow,
  red and beige
Two buttons for eyes
Dressmakers' pattern paper
Dressmakers' carbon paper
Matching threads

THE NEST
½yd (40cm) of 36in (90cm) wide
  turquoise cotton fabric
6in (15cm) of 36in (90cm) wide
  ecru cotton fabric
20in (50cm) square of light-
  weight padding
5yd (4.4m) of ⅜in (1cm) wide ribbon

Dressmakers' pattern paper
Dressmakers' carbon paper
Matching and contrasting
  threads
14in (36cm) cushion pad

LEAF CUSHION
1yd (1m) of 36in (90cm) wide
  black sateen
½yd (40cm) of 36in (90cm) wide
  ecru sateen
Suitable filling for the motif

Dressmakers' pattern paper
Dressmakers' carbon paper
Matching threads
12in (30cm) cushion pad

CIRCULAR CUSHION
⅝yd (50cm) of 36in (90cm) wide
  ecru cotton fabric
⅝yd (50cm) of 40in (100cm) wide
  light-weight polyester padding
  (optional)

Pencil or tailors' chalk
14in (36cm) diameter circle of
  1½in (4cm) thick foam

DIRECTIONS

THE HEN
▦ Draw up the patterns for the hen, beak, comb and wattle from the diagram, marking in the lines for the feathers and eyes. Cut out as stated and mark design on right side of one pair of hen shapes.

▦ From beige fabric cut out two 1in (2.5cm) diameter circles for eyes. Place each eye on one of a pair of hen shapes; pin, tack and zigzag stitch in place. Stitch a button into the center of each beige eye.

▦ Place a layer of padding behind two hen shapes and, using colors stated, embroider

with humor and flair

the features and wings using a close zigzag stitch on a sewing machine. It may help if you back the padding with tissue paper, to be pulled away after machining.

▦ Place comb and wattle pieces in pairs with wrong sides together; pin, tack and zigzag stitch together around the outer edge. Repeat to make up beak from yellow fabric. Lay the pieces on the right side of one hen shape, matching edges where they will join. Pin, tack and stitch pieces to hen shape.

▦ Place hen shapes with right sides together. Pin, tack and stitch together, taking a ⅝in (1.5cm) seam allowance and catching in beak, comb and wattle. Leave base open. Turn right side out.

▦ Stitch the two remaining hen shapes together, again leaving base open. Insert into decorated hen. Turn edges in to meet each other around base opening: pin, tack and topstitch close to edge.

THE NEST

▦ Draw up the pattern from the diagram, marking in straw lines.

▦ From turquoise fabric cut out two cushion pieces, each 15¼in (39cm) square. Cut a piece of padding the same size.

▦ Transfer the design to one cushion piece and pin and tack padding behind it. Using a close zigzag stitch, work in the straw lines in lime and blue.

▦ From ecru cotton fabric cut out three eggs. Repeat, to cut eggs from padding. Pin and tack to wrong side of fabric eggs. Place eggs in the center of the cushion, overlapping each other. Pin, tack and zigzag stitch.

▦ Place cushion pieces with right sides together, raw edges matching; pin, tack and stitch together all around, leaving an opening in the center of one side, for turning. Trim and turn to right side. Insert cushion pad. Turn in opening edges and slipstitch.

▦ Cut ribbon into two 24in (60cm) lengths and two 64in (160cm) lengths. Handstitch the center of each length to each corner, with larger ties placed at the front.

1 square = 2in x 2in

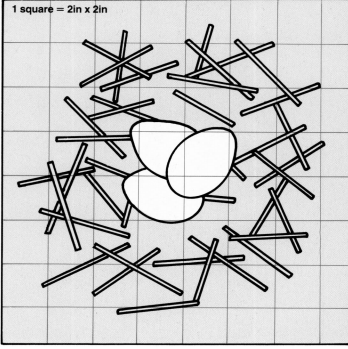

1 square = 2in x 2in

CIRCULAR CUSHION

▦ From fabric cut out two 15¼in (39cm) diameter circles. For the gusset, measure around the cushion ⅝in (1.5cm) in from the edge and cut one piece to this length plus 1¼in (3cm) seam allowance and 2¾in (7cm) wide.

▦ If using padding, cut one circle and one gusset, without seam allowances, from padding, and pin and tack to back of one fabric circle and gusset.

▦ Staystitch all around the circles, ⅝in (1.5cm) from the outer edge. Snip into the seam allowance up to the stitching. With right sides together, pin, tack and stitch the gusset together into a ring. Position gusset around one circle (if using padding, pin to padded circle). Pin, tack and stitch together around line of stay-stitching.

▦ Mark in lines for decorative stitching across the cushion and gusset with a pencil or tailors'

1 square = 2in x 2in

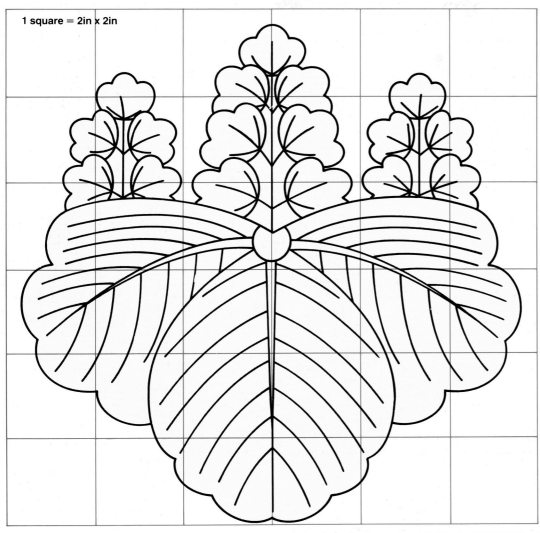

THE LEAF CUSHION

▦ Draw up the design from the diagram, including all the design lines.

▦ From black sateen cut out two pieces each 13¼in (33cm) square. From ecru sateen cut out one leaf arrangement and transfer design lines to the motif.

▦ Position the leaf arrangement centrally on one cushion piece. Using matching thread, pin and tack around, taking small stitches and adding a small amount of filling as you work. When

complete, zigzag stitch around the design. Then zigzag stitch the design lines using black thread.

▦ Place the two cushion cover pieces with right sides together; pin, tack and stitch together all around, leaving a central opening in one side. Trim and turn to right side. Insert cushion pad; turn in opening edges and slipstitch together to close.

chalk. Work a tight zigzag stitch over the marked decorative lines.

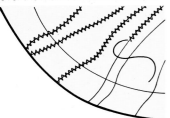

▦ Place second cushion cover piece to opposite edge of gusset with right sides together. Pin, tack and stitch together, leaving an opening. Trim and turn to right side. Insert foam rubber; turn in opening edges in line with the remainder of the seam; slipstitch together to close.

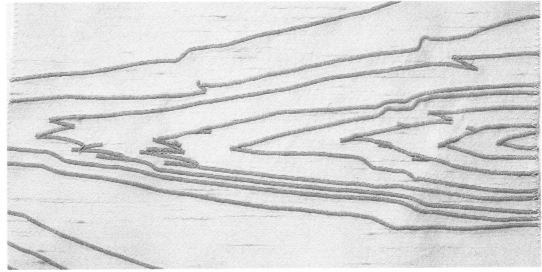

SLEEPING CAT AND DOG

Getting children to go to bed can be quite a problem, especially in long summer-holiday evenings, but you'll find it a whole lot easier with the help of these cheerful sleeping bags. Although they may look as if they entail a lot of work, they are in fact relatively quick and simple to make. Choose suitably doggy or catlike material, with a striped or spotted pattern, and – most important of all – washable.

MATERIALS

For either bag:
7⅔yd (7m) of 36in (90cm) wide striped or spotted cotton fabric
4yd (3.5m) of 36in (90cm) wide muslin
40in (100cm) wide heavyweight polyester padding, 8oz (200g)
4½yd (4m) for the cat or 4yd

(3.5m) for the dog
20in (50cm) square of plain black cotton fabric (dog only)
Dressmakers' pattern paper
Dressmakers' carbon paper
Embroidery cottons
Matching threads

DIRECTIONS

FOR EITHER ANIMAL

▧ Draw up pattern from diagram and cut out from stated fabrics, adding a ⅝in (1.5cm) seam allowance around each fabric piece and padding pieces for main body and for the head pieces.

▧ Make the fore and hind legs in the same way: place the two pieces of each limb with right sides together, raw edges aligned; pin, tack and stitch all around, leaving the edge that will join to body open. Trim and turn to right side. Insert padding; pin, tack and stitch across open edges. Topstitch each limb as indicated.

▧ For the tail, cut a strip of fabric 28in (70cm) long and 8in (20cm) wide and, folded right sides together, join across one end and down long side. Cut strip of padding to match, roll it up and unfold tail, right side out, over padding. Pin, tack and stitch across top end.

▧ Place one body front to muslin, sandwiching padding in between. Pin, tack and topstitch across body, following stripes (on cat) or rows of spots (dog) as a guide. Stop short at the seamline, ⅝in (1.5cm) in from the raw edges. Repeat for back body.

▧ For each body piece, stitch

through all three layers along seamline right around the edge, then trim back edge of padding close to seamline. Lay the legs and tail on top of front body, matching edges at the points where limbs join body. Pin, tack and stitch in position, still lying inwards.

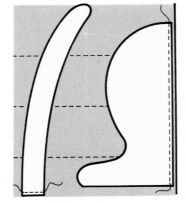

▧ Pin back body to front, right sides facing, leaving top edge free. Tack and then stitch all around, catching in legs and tail.

▧ Dog's ears: place each pair of ear pieces right sides together. Pin, tack and stitch around outer edge, leaving joining edge open. Turn right side out, insert padding, then topstitch by hand to hold padding in place, stitching close to outer edge all around. Pin, tack and stitch straight across open edge.

46

cosy pets to snuggle with

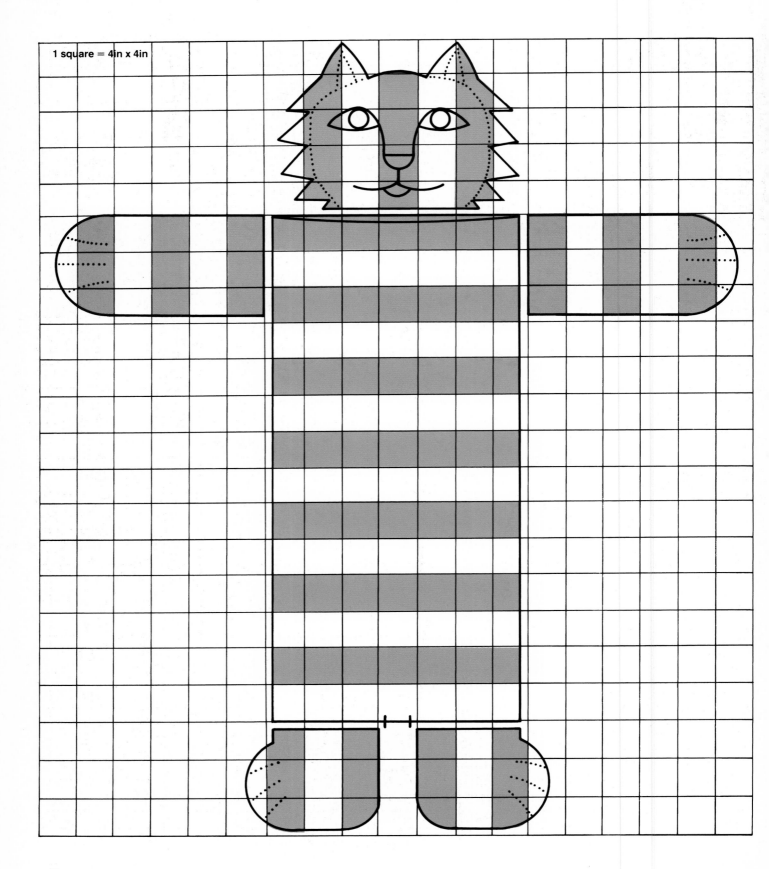

1 square = 4in x 4in

▦ Using carbon paper, lightly mark in features on one head piece. Place on a layer of padding backed by a layer of muslin. Embroider features in straight stitch, either by hand or machine.

▦ For dog, lay ears on front head, lying inwards and matching joining edges.

▦ For either bag, place back head with right sides to front head; pin, tack and stitch together, leaving neck edge free. Trim padding from seam allowance and turn head right side out. Insert second layer of padding, then pin, tack and stitch straight across neck edge.

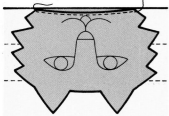

▦ Place head on right side of back body, matching neck edge with center of top edge of body. Pin and tack in place.

▦ Make up the bag lining from two remaining body pieces: place with right sides together; pin, tack and stitch around, leaving top edge open and a central opening in base edge. Place lining over sleeping bag with right sides together, top edges matching. Pin, tack and stitch all around top edge, catching in head.

▦ Pull up lining and turn in opening edge, in line with remainder of seam; pin, tack and stitch to close. Push lining down inside bag.

▦ If desired, add a fabric tie to the end of the tail and a button to the base, so the bag can be rolled up and tied.

1 square = 4in x 4in

49

CHILD'S COMFORTER

Turn a pattern of big, bold squares to your advantage by using it to provide the outlines for a quilt with the visual effect of patchwork. The quilting is worked by hand but with long, quick stitches which are meant to be noticed. The intersections are emphasized with tufts which also help to hold the padding in place. The result is a cosy, stylish quilt – just the thing to keep a child warm (and asleep) on a cold night. But because it is so quick to make, it won't break your heart to see it jumped on, rolled up and sat on or subjected to the inevitable accidents of childhood.

Finished size: 57in × 47in (144cm × 118cm), though the size can easily be adjusted to suit your needs or to fit in with the size of the pattern of your chosen fabric

MATERIALS

1¾yd (1.5m) of 48in (120cm) wide squared fabric	heavy-weight padding
1¾yd (1.5m) of 48in (120cm) wide striped fabric	Heavy cotton thread for quilting and knots
2¾yd (2.4m) of 36in (90cm) wide	Matching threads

DIRECTIONS

▦ From squared fabric cut out one piece 58¼in × 47¾in (147cm × 120cm), which includes ⅝in (1.5cm) all around for seam allowance. Repeat, to cut a piece the same size from the striped fabric.

▦ Place the two fabric pieces with right sides together. Pin, tack and stitch together all around, leaving a 28in (70cm) central opening in one short side. Stitch around quilt again close to previous row of stitches. Trim and turn the 'bag' around to right side.

▦ Cut out two 46½in (117cm) lengths of padding. Align the long edges closely against each other and herringbone stitch along the joining. Turn the padding over and herringbone stitch over the joining on the opposite side. Trim the width down to 57in (144cm) with the seam centrally placed. Insert the padding inside the cover. Turn in the opening edges in line with the remainder of the seam and slipstitch together to close.

▦ Quilt the cover by hand along the squares of the design, as shown in the diagram, taking about ⅝in (1.5cm) per stitch. If your fabric has larger or smaller squares, you may have to adapt the quilting pattern slightly, but make sure that the lines are close enough to hold the layers,

▦ Make tufts of thread at each intersection: thread a needle with two or three lengths of heavy cotton thread. Push the needle through the quilt slightly to one side of the intersection and bring it up the same distance from the intersection on the opposite side. Tie the threads together over the intersection with a square knot. Trim ends to 1¼in (3cm).

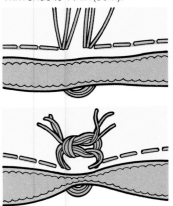

Make up the comforter from two different layers of fabric, pick one striped and one squared, so that you can flip it over on different days to change the look of the bed. Held inside by the handstitched quilting is a warm layer of padding – follow the design lines of the fabric when stitching.

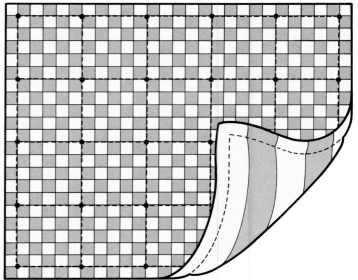

quick and easy quilt

MIDNIGHT MONSTERS

Your children will love these friendly prehistoric sleeping bags, and they'll probably be able to tell you the names of the dinosaurs without looking them up. Just to remind you, they are: dimetrodon (green), protoceratops (blue) and triceratops (maroon). Although they look impressively complicated, they are not all that difficult to make, especially as the quilting, which can be worked by hand or machine, is intended to produce an authentically wrinkled-looking surface. The edges are also easy to finish; they are covered with bias binding.

MATERIALS

FOR EACH BAG

2¼yd (2.2m) of 45in (115cm) wide cotton for back, in color of your choice
4¼yd (3.8m) of 39in (100cm) wide heavy-weight polyester padding (if your machine cannot take heavy-weight padding, use the medium weight)
Fusible webbing
Quilting threads
Dressmakers' pattern paper
Matching threads

In addition you will also need:

DIMETRODON

6½yd (6m) of 45in (115cm) wide percale or glazed cotton in green
⅝yd (50cm) as above in navy
7¼yd (6.6m) of ¾in (2cm) wide
bias binding in green and 1⅝yd (1.5m) in navy
Scrap of pale yellow cotton fabric

PROTOCERATOPS

5yd (4.5m) of 45in (115cm) wide percale or glazed cotton in blue
1¾yd (1.6m) as above in blue gray
5yd (4.6m) of ¾in (2cm) wide bias
binding in blue gray and 2¾yd (2.5m) in blue
Scraps of pale yellow and pink cotton fabrics

TRICERATOPS

6½yd (5.8m) of 45in (115cm) wide maroon percale or glazed cotton
8½yd (7.6m) of ¾in (2cm) wide maroon bias binding
Scrap of pale yellow fabric

DIRECTION

DIMETRODON

▦ Scale up the pattern on to dressmakers' pattern paper and cut one complete outline in cotton and one in green percale or glazed cotton. They must make a matching pair (with wrong sides together). If you are making two bags and want the heads of finished bags to face each other when your children are using them, bear this in mind when cutting. Also cut one whole outline from padding.
▦ Cut along neckline of pattern and cut out one whole body only from percale and one from padding (the percale should lie wrong side up in same direction as previous pieces).
▦ Cut along lines between upper and lower body and tail. Cut out body top in green percale. Adding ⅜in (1cm) along division between body top and bottom but not along outer edge, cut belly and tail from blue percale.

dinosaurs with a difference

▦ Cut out out eye in yellow fabric and fusible webbing. Iron webbing to back of eye then position eye on head. Iron in place then zigzag stitch.

▦ Place head-and-body pieces wrong sides together, sandwiching padding in between. Pin and tack. With navy thread, quilt features on head.

▦ Lay body piece wrong side up. Place padding on top, matching outer edges. Place upper body section over two lower body pieces, overlapping them by ⅜in (1cm). Pin and tack, then place on top of padding and lining. Pin and tack all three together.

▦ Zigzag stitch, along line between upper and lower body. Quilt features in navy and yellow.

▦ Fold green binding evenly over neck edge. Pin, tack and topstitch.

▦ Position front on back with wrong sides together, matching outer edges. Pin, tack and stitch together close to edge all around. Bind outer edge, as neck edge.

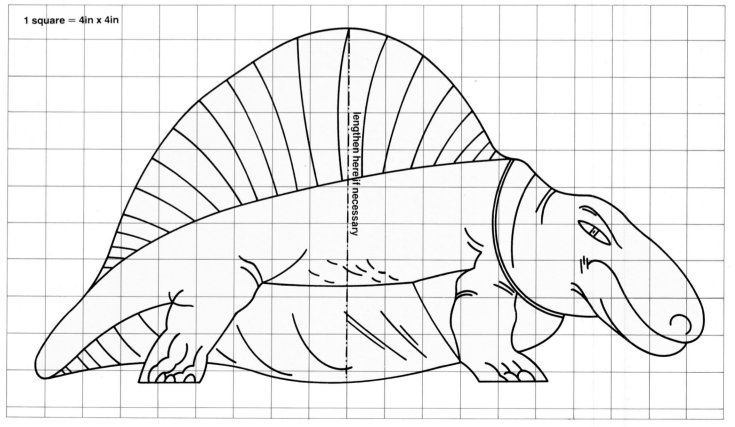

1 square = 4in x 4in

lengthen here if necessary

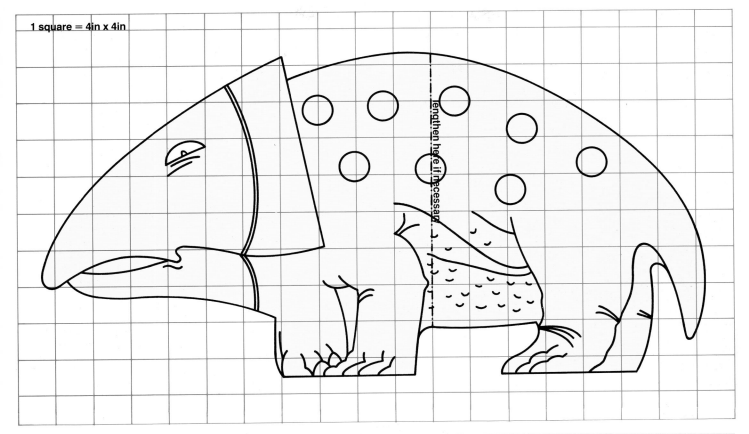

1 square = 4in x 4in

lengthen here if necessary

PROTOCERATOPS

▨ Make up the back in the same way as for dimetrodon, this time adding a pale yellow eye and pink mouth to a head-and-body piece of blue percale.

▨ Cut out body section from blue percale and from padding, then in blue gray, minus collar piece, and adding ⅜in (1cm) along line where collar will meet body. From blue, cut collar piece. Also cut section between front legs (do not add allowance). Pin and tack inter-leg section in place on blue gray body and overlap and tack collar to body.

▨ From fusible webbing cut out eight 2½in (6cm) diameter spots. Place on wrong side of navy fabric and iron in place. Cut out spots, place on front body and iron in place.

▨ Put the three layers of body section together. Zigzag stitch around spots, neckline and inter-leg section and quilt features, then bind neck and outer edges as for dimetrodon.

TRICERATOPS

▦ This is made in the same way as the two previous animals.

▦ If you do not like the sloping neck edge or feel that it will not be effectively wide enough for a larger child, you can carry the opening on down the outer line of the front leg.

▦ If the bag also needs to be wider, fill in the spaces between the legs with grass green or sand fabric to produce a straight edge down that side.

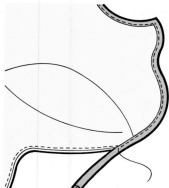

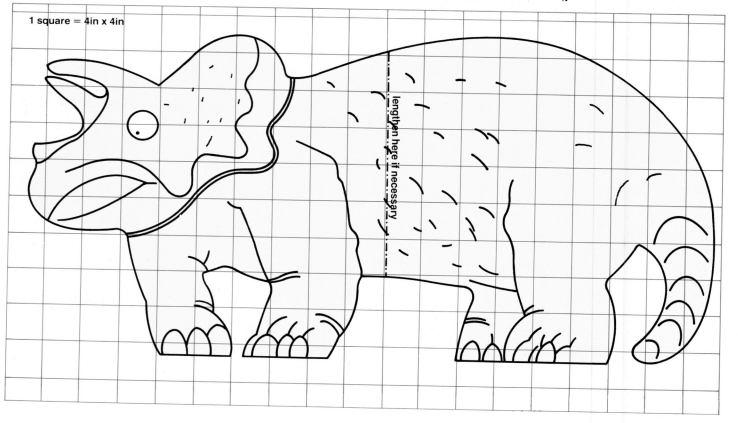

1 square = 4in x 4in

lengthen here if necessary

TWEED BLANKET

Irish tweeds provide a rich and unusual patchwork fabric. This luxuriously warm blanket, with its warm blend of natural, earthy colors, would look equally at home in a country cottage or an ultra-modern setting. Although these heavier fabrics are not as easy to make up into patchwork as the more commonly used cottons, there is no great difficulty in joining these large-scale uncomplicated patches. If you don't want to buy the tweeds, use rummage sale findings (if the fabric is still in good condition) or ask tailoring shops if you can have their old sample books.

Finished size: the blanket can be as large or as small as you desire

MATERIALS

An assortment of different colored tweed fabrics
Piece of flannelette sheeting for interlining (optional)

Piece of tweed or heavy brushed cotton the finished size for backing and the borders
Matching threads

DIRECTIONS

▦ Cut out a 6in (15cm) square template from card, making sure that each corner is a right angle. Using this template mark and cut out squares from each of the tweed fabrics, allowing a ⅜in (1cm) seam allowance all around.

▦ Lay all the squares out on the floor and move them about until you have the desired effect, then pile them up in order in rows. Number rows by pinning a piece of paper to the top of each pile.

▦ Begin by joining the squares together to form widthways rows: place the first two squares with right sides together; pin, tack and stitch. Repeat to stitch all the squares together to complete the first row. Trim and press seams open. Repeat for each row.

▦ Place the first two rows with right sides together; pin, tack and stitch together, making sure that the seams match. Repeat, until one half of the patchwork is made, then join up the other half. Finish by sewing the two halves together.

▦ Cut and join flannelette sheeting, if using, and tweed backing to the size of the finished patchwork plus an extra 3¼in (8.5cm) all around. Lay the sheeting on the wrong side of the backing: pin, tack and stitch, using an ordinary running stitch and sewing ⅝in (1.5cm) from edges.

▦ Center the patchwork over the sheeting and, in the same way, pin, tack and stitch all around, ⅝in (1.5cm) in from edge of the patchwork.

▦ For a border, cut two strips of tweed 9in (23cm) wide to the length of the blanket backing plus 1¼in (3cm) and two to the width plus 1¼in. At the end of each strip, fold up the edges and bring the corners together, forming a miter. Press, then cut along pressed line, checking that lines slope evenly.

▦ Place strips together in order: pin, tack and stitch across shaped ends to within ⅝in (1.5cm) of edges. Press seams open.

▦ Place border frame to right side of patchwork: pin, tack and stitch.

▦ Fold border over to enclose all raw edges and slipstitch in position at the back.

SEMINOLE PATCHWORK

This intricately patterned patchwork would be the focal point of any room setting: drape it over a bed or table, display it as a wall hanging, or expand the size with extra squares and make a room divider. Although it looks dauntingly complex and difficult to sew, appearances are deceptive, for it is made up by a simple machine technique invented by the Seminole Indians of southern Florida . . . Instead of cutting and sewing each patch separately, the secret is to machine stitch long strips of fabric together – the strips are then cut across and reassembled, producing an elaborate mosaic effect with the minimum of effort.

Finished size: 50½in (128cm) square.

MATERIALS

36in (90cm) wide cotton fabric as
   follows:
1⅝yd (1.5m) in ochre
1yd (1m) in prune
⅞yd (80cm) in brick
¾yd (70cm) in brown
¾yd (70cm) in rose pink
⅝yd (50cm) in beige

4in (10cm) in khaki
1½yd (1.4m) of 54in (137cm)
   wide cotton fabric, for backing
⅝yd (50cm) of 54in (137cm) wide
   cotton fabric in blue, for border
Matching threads

DIRECTIONS

▦ The patchwork quilt is made up of sixteen squares, each 10⅝in (27cm) in size. Each square has a different arrangement of fabrics, chosen from the seven used for the project.

▦ There are two basic techniques used for the squares. In the first, two fabrics are cut up into equal-width strips. These strips are then stitched together, alternating the two colors. The resulting piece is then cut up into equal-sized strips, the cuts running at right angles to the strips. This produces new strips, made of patchwork, which are then aligned to form a building brick arrangement, before being stitched together and trimmed to form the final square. This method can also be used with three or four different colored fabrics, to produce a chequer-board arrangement.

American Indian designs

 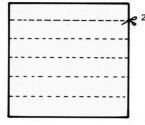 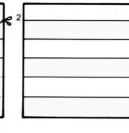 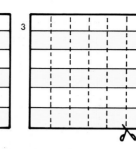 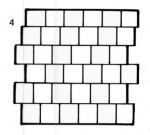

1 Take two or more pieces of fabric and trim them to the same size.

2 Join the strips together taking ¼in (6mm) seams and alternating the colors.

3 Mark lines across the piece of strip patchwork, at right angles to the bands of color, and cut along the marked lines.

4 Assemble the patchwork strips to make a stepped pattern and join taking ¼in (6mm) seams. Trim uneven edges.

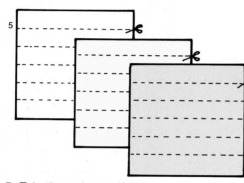 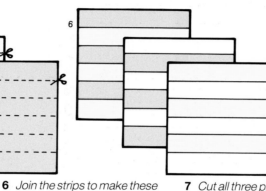 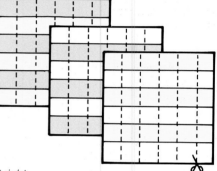

5 Take three pieces of fabric, all the same size, and mark and cut them into strips.

6 Join the strips to make these different two-color patchwork pieces.

7 Cut all three pieces at right angles to the strips of color. Assemble the patchwork strips to make a chequer-board pattern.

 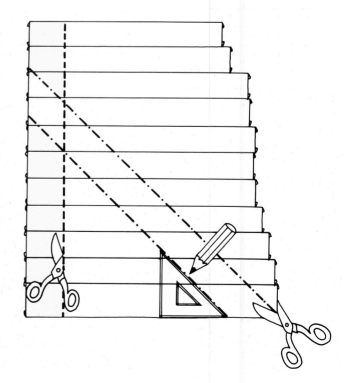

In the second technique, the fabrics are again cut into strips and joined to make a piece of strip patchwork. This time, however, instead of cutting at right angles across the strips, the cuts are made at an angle to produce strips of diamond-shaped patches. Using a set square, mark across the piece of strip patchwork at an angle of 45 degrees either to the left or to the right. In each case the strips of patchwork are aligned to achieve a diagonal effect. The two strips with the patches running in opposite directions can be joined together to create a chevron effect.

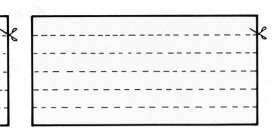

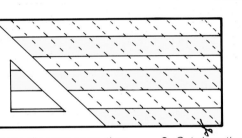

1 *For diamond and chevron patterns, take two fabrics. Press them and trim away any selvedges. Mark both fabrics in strips of equal width. Cut along the lines and then join the strips together, alternating the colors and taking ¼in (6mm) seam allowances.*

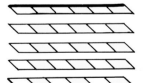

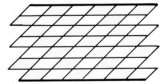

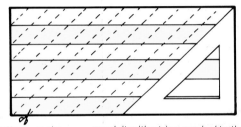
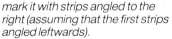

2 *Press all seams open, then mark off strips at an angle of 45° to the previous ones.*

3 *Cut along the marked lines and pile them up, maintaining the color order.*

4 *For a chevron pattern, make up a second, identical piece of straight-strip patchwork, then*

mark it with strips angled to the right (assuming that the first strips angled leftwards).

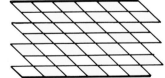

5 *Cut along the strips of second piece, keeping them separate from the first pile.*

6 *The bands from the second piece of patchwork can form left-leaning diamonds.*

7 *The bands from the first piece making right-leaning diamonds, as in square J.*

8 *Bands from both pieces alternate to form a chevron pattern.*

Following these two techniques make up the squares in the following way. Remember to add a ¼in (6cm) seam allowance to the strip measurements and cut all strips 22in (45cm) long.

A – Use technique 1 in prune and pink. Cut out 1¾in (4.5cm) wide strips of fabric each time.

B – Use technique 2 in prune and ochre. Cut out 1¼in (3cm) wide strips, then cut diagonally to the right, making 2¼in (5.5cm) wide bands.

C – Use technique 1 in ochre, beige and pink. Cut out 1¼in (3cm) wide strips each time.

D – Use technique 2 in prune and beige. Cut out 1¼in (3cm) wide strips, then cut a mixture of left and right diagonal strips into 1½in (4cm) wide bands.

E – Make up this square in the same way, in prune and brown, as square D, but cutting 2¼in (5.5cm) wide bands.

F – Make up this square in the same way, in ochre and brick, as square D, but cut out ¾in (2cm) wide strips and make up 2¼in (6cm) wide bands.

G – Make up this square in the same way, in ochre and brown, as square D, but cut out 1¾in (4.5cm) wide strips and make up 2¼in (6cm) wide bands.

H – Make up this square in the same way, in pink and beige, as square D, but cut out 1¼in (3cm) wide strips and make up into 2in (5cm) wide bands.

I – For this square use technique 1, in beige and ochre. Cut out 1in (2.5cm) wide strips each time.

J – For this square use technique 2, in brick and prune. Cut out 1¼in (3.5cm) wide strips, then cut diagonally to the left into 2¼in (5.5cm) wide bands.

K – Use technique 1 for this square in prune, khaki, pink and brown. Cut out 1½in (4cm) wide strips each time.

L – Make up this square in the same way, in ochre and prune, as square J, but cut out 1¾in (4.5cm) wide strips each time.

M – Make up this square in the same way in pink and beige, as square D, but cut out 1in (2.5cm) wide strips and make up into 1¾in (4.5cm) wide bands.

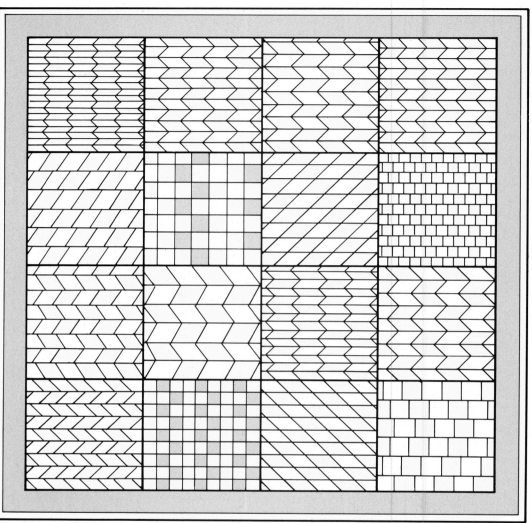

N – Make up this square in the same way, in ochre and brown, as square D, but cut out 1¼in (3cm) wide strips and make them up into 2¼in (6cm) wide bands.

O – Make up this square in the same way, in prune and brown, as square D, but cut out 1in (2.5cm) wide strips and make up into 2¼in (5.5cm) wide bands.

P – Make up this square in the same way, in ochre and brick, as square D, but cut out ⅝in (1.5cm) wide strips and make them up into 5.5cm (2¼in) wide bands.

When all the squares are complete, pin and stitch them together in the correct order, following the diagram, with right sides together and taking ¼in (6mm) wide seam allowances.

For the border, cut out two strips of blue fabric, each 43in × 4¾in (109cm × 12cm) for top and bottom of quilt. Place each strip with right side to patchwork; pin and stitch, taking ¼in (6mm) seam allowances. Fold down the border strips with right sides up. From blue fabric cut out two strips, each 51½in × 4¾in (131cm × 12cm) for sides. Position each strip to the remaining sides of the patchwork, with right sides together. Pin and stitch in place. Fold down the border strips with right sides up.

From backing fabric cut out one piece 54in (137cm) square. Place to patchwork with wrong sides together; pin and tack all round. Turn 1¼in (3cm) wide border of backing fabric over to the right side of the quilt; turn under ¼in (6mm). Pin and stitch.

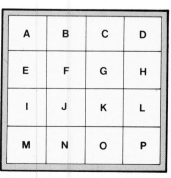

After making up each individual square, stitch them together in the above order to achieve the quilt.

WHITE HANGING

Hunting through the fabrics in junk shops or at rummage sales, you will sometimes find old sheets or pillowcases, perhaps decorated with delicate embroideries, which are too beautiful to throw away but too worn for practical use. Here's a way to take the unworn sections and the pretty, embroidered motifs, and extract the maximum visual pleasure from them by turning them into a romantic but sophisticated wall hanging, a patchwork of antiques. If you have no monogrammed items, work your own embroidered initials.

Finished size: 148in × 61in (121cm × 155cm)

MATERIALS

2⅛yd (2m) of 48in (120cm) wide fine, closely woven white cotton or linen, preferably old, but not too worn sheeting
1⅞yd (1.7m) of 48in (120cm) wide white cotton fabric, for lining
5yd (4.5m) of 40in (100cm) wide

light-weight polyester padding
Well-sharpened light-colored pencil
Lead pencil
Tracing paper
Dressmaker's carbon paper
Matching thread

On all the quilting squares, place the top fabric with wrong side to lining, sandwiching the padding in between. Adjust the sewing machine by loosening the tension and set the stitch length to a medium-size stitch. Quilt over the marked lines of each design in turn, using a quilting foot-and guide bar to obtain evenly spaced lines of stitching. Begin and end the stitching ⅝in (1.5cm) from all the raw edges. Begin by stitching the center lines and then work out from the center in either direction.

For the embroidered squares: trace off the chosen initials, adding flowers and bows, as desired. Center the tracing right side up on the fabric square and pin at each corner. Slide a piece of carbon paper face downwards between the tracing and the fabric. Mark over the design lines. Work each motif in padded satin stitch. Add a row of cross stitches as desired.

When each embroidered square is complete, place a layer of padding and then a layer of lining fabric and pin and tack together.

To stitch the squares together, start by joining them into rows. Place squares with right sides together, then pin, tack and stitch through all layers. Trim padding right back to stitching line to reduce bulk. Lightly press seams open. At each side of seam, turn top fabric and lining seam allowances in by ¼in (6mm) to meet each other and sew together with running stitch, by hand or machine. Lightly catchstitch the seam allowances to the lining to hold them flat.

DIRECTIONS

From white cotton or linen fabric cut out twelve 14¾in (37cm) squares. Repeat with padding and lining. Fold each square in half both ways and press to mark the center point.

For squares C, H, I and K mark the design straight on the fabric using a well-sharpened pencil in a light color, following the diagram. Working from the center point using a ruler mark out the lines for squares C, H and I. Use a shell

around. Adhere tracing to thin card and cut around the outline with a craft knife. Mark from the center out both ways untill the square is complete.

For squares A and F, it will be necessary to draw up the design first. Mark the correct size square on a sheet of paper and, using a compass and pencil, mark out each design. Transfer to the fabric: place the design centrally on the right side of the fabric and pin at

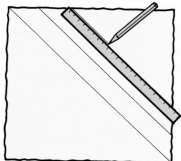

template for square K. To make the template, trace over the template given here. Cut around the tracing, leaving a border of approximately ¾in (2cm) all

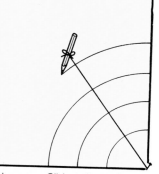

each corner. Slide a sheet of carbon paper, face downwards, between paper and fabric; trace out the design with a pencil or a tracing wheel.

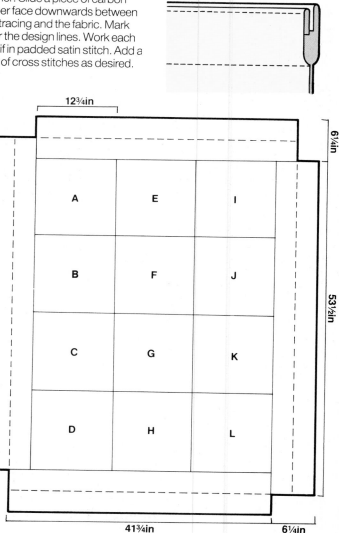

the elegance of antique linens

Machine quilting requires a certain degree of practice and skill and you may find that some of the quilting patterns shown here, especially those with curves, are too difficult for you. If so, you could either repeat some of the straight line patterns instead, or work quilting by hand. The squares would be easier to quilt in a hoop if you marked them out on a single piece of fabric, assembled the three layers of padding, backing and top fabric together, and then cut the squares apart after quilting.

Squares **B, D, E, G, J** and **L** are unquilted and have embroidered initials, along the lines of the two examples given on the right.

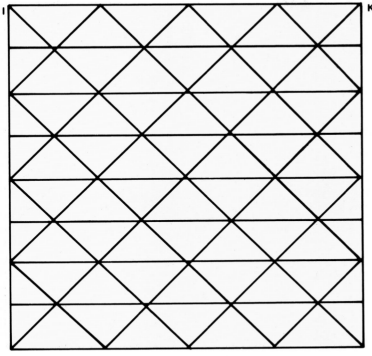

▦ When all rows are complete, join them together in the same manner as the squares.

▦ For the borders cut two strips for the side edges, each 55in × 9in (139cm × 22cm) and two strips each 49½in × 9in (124cm × 22cm) for top and base edges. Pin, tack and stitch one edge of side strips to each side of hanging taking a ⅝in (1.5cm) seam allowance. Fold in half, turn under seam allowance and slipstitch remaining long edge to reverse side of hanging over previous stitches.

▦ Repeat, to bind the bottom edge in the same way, stitching across the side strips to form neat corners. Slipstitch up the side edges of borders. Bind the top edge in the same way, but leave the side edges open to form a casing for a hanging pole.

CRAZY COVER

If you enjoy going to extremes when it comes to lavishly embellished and ornate surroundings, make yourself a richly patterned and textured cover along the lines of this antique crazy quilt. The Victorians called this type of work crazy patchwork because the patches are completely random and can be decorated with anything that comes to hand – signatures, sentimental mementoes, ribbons, buttons and, of course, embroidery stitches. So raid your wardrobe, cut up all your outdated evening dresses and start sewing!

MATERIALS

Assortment of scraps or remnants of various fabrics – silks, velvets, brocades or cottons
Background fabric in light-weight calico or cotton, sufficient for the desired size of cover
Backing fabric of cotton to line the finished patchwork
Embroidery cottons in different colors
Matching threads

DIRECTIONS

▦ The patchwork can either be sewn as one piece or, to make it easier to handle, in squares or rectangles of manageable size which can be joined together when the work is complete.

▦ Start by cutting patches and dividing them into colors and shades so that you can make sure that you have a good blend as you progress. Remember that they will be much smaller once you have overlapped them and turned under raw edges. Avoid sharp points or tight curves.

▦ If some of the patches which you wish to use are rather small, join them together to make more usable strips.

▦ If you are making the cover in sections, cut the background fabric into squares or rectangles, making sure that they are all the same size.

▦ Whether you are working the whole cover or sections, begin by positioning a right-angled patch on one corner of the background fabric and pinning. Work across from this point, adding further patches to cover the raw edges of the previous ones and overlapping by at least ⅜in (1cm). It helps to work on a large flat surface and to leave all patches but the first unpinned until you are happy that you have a really attractive combination of colors and tones.

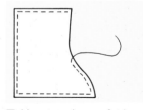

▦ Use your pieces of strip patchwork to cover long raw edges and provide a contrast in size.

▦ When the backing fabric is covered and you have checked that no small areas of it are showing through, pin all the patches in position.

▦ There are several ways of sewing the patches in position. The quickest method is to tack down the patches without turning the edges under and then sew them with a machine zigzag stitch, covering raw edges.

▦ The more traditional method, and the one which you should use if you intend to combine the patchwork with hand embroidery stitches, as on the example shown here, is to turn under and tack overlapping edges and then sew them with either a small

wildly luxurious Victorian patchwork

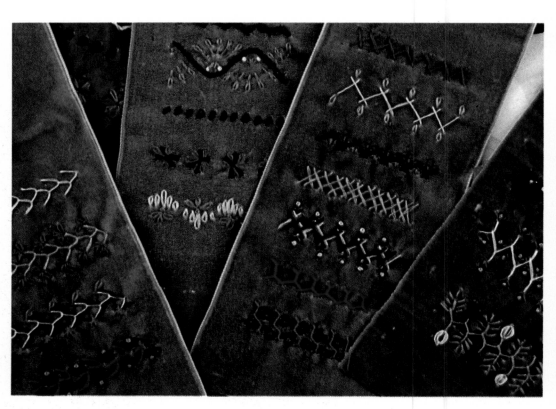

running stitch or a blind stitch. If the embroidery stitch is dense enough, then you can simply embroider the patches in position. If not, embroider after the patches have been handsewn or machine stitched on to the backing fabric.

▦ Leave raw edges at the outer edge of the work. If you are working in sections, trim completed sections to the same size then join them with a ⅜in (1cm) seam, sewing through all layers. Press seams open.

▦ Cut and join strips of the backing fabric to make a piece large enough to back the cover. Either cut the backing to the same size as the work, sew around the edge with right sides together and leaving an opening, turn right side out and slipstitch to close, or make a self binding. To do this, cut the backing 2½in (6.5cm) larger than the patchwork all around. With wrong sides together, lay the top over the backing. Turn under raw edge of backing by ⅝in (1.5cm) then bring it over raw edge of top, folding in a miter at the corners, and topstitch in position.

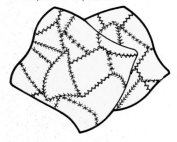

If you don't have the time to make a full-scale cover like the one shown here, why not make something smaller and more manageable, at least to start with? The Victorians used crazy quilting for various small objects such as cushions and tea cosies, firescreens or small tablecloths.

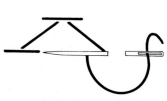

1 Basic cross stitch

2 Basic feather stitch

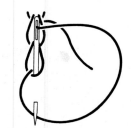

3 Basic chainstitch

4 Herringbone

5 Open Cretan stitch

6 Feathered chainstitch

7 Blanket stitch, chevron stitch

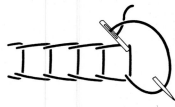

8 Closed buttonhole stitch

9 Square chainstitch

AMERICAN DREAM

The themes used in this charming wall hanging are quintessentially American – block patchwork, album quilts and blue jeans – a visual tribute to the pioneers of the Midwest. Block patterns, so called because the patchwork was divided up into easily manageable blocks, are very characteristic of American work. Sometimes, perhaps to celebrate a wedding, a group of friends and relatives would meet together to make an album quilt, like this one: each person would make a different block and then they would have a party at which the blocks would be joined together and quilted.

Finished size: the work can be as large or as small as you want – or feel you have time for

MATERIALS

Assorted scraps of calico and denim fabrics	Squared graph paper
Backing fabric	Card and craft knife
Light-weight polyester padding	Colored pencils and lead pencil
	Matching threads

DIRECTIONS

▦ The patchwork is made up of blocks with four squares across and four down, alternated with plain squares, making five blocks or plain squares across and five down. Patchwork blocks normally measure between 8in (20cm) and 15in (36cm) across, so the finished piece could measure from 39in (100cm) to 73in (185cm) either way (not counting borders). Each small square could therefore measure from 2in (5cm) to 3½in (9cm) each way.

▦ When you have decided how large you wish the work to be, draw a small square to full scale on graph paper and divide it diagonally into two triangles. Draw up another triangle to the same scale and add a ¼in (6mm) seam allowance all around.

▦ Cut out one triangle without allowance and one with, leaving

some extra space all around, and adhere to card, then cut out along the pencil lines with a craft knife to make two templates.

▦ Using colored pencils, make a small-scale drawing of the finished work, then use it to work out how many triangles you will need from each fabric. Using the larger template, and a colored pencil, mark out the appropriate number of patches on each fabric.

▦ Using the smaller template and leaving an even space all around, mark out the inner, sewing line on each patch, then cut out patches. If you are sewing by machine, you need not mark the sewing line as you can use the outer edge of the presser foot as a guide or else stick a length of masking tape on the throat plate, ¼in (6mm) away from the needle.

▦ Arrange the fabric triangles into geometric patterns of your choice or according to the picture. The

With triangles as the base, even using only two fabrics – calico and denim – design ideas are endless. When stitching the triangles together to make up the squares, just remember to carefully match up the seams, as bad joins will

spoil the look of the quilt, and the square produced will be off grain. After stitching, press all the seam allowance to one side, before working the next seam.

patchwork wall hanging

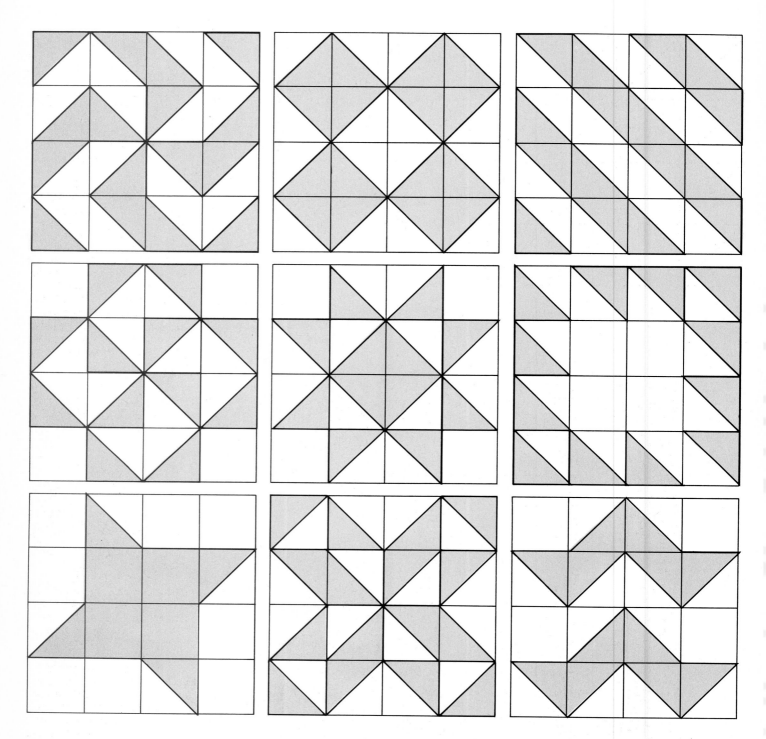

Use these blocks to calculate how much fabric you will need in each color. Draw each on graph paper and shade in the colors of your choice then work out the total number of patches you will need in each fabric. Remembering to add seam allowances, and bearing in mind you can fit two triangles together to make a square, divide the width of your fabric, less selvedges, by the width of a patch, to find out how many patches you can fit across the width of your fabric. Use this to work out the length of fabric required in each color, adding a small amount for possible mistakes during cutting.

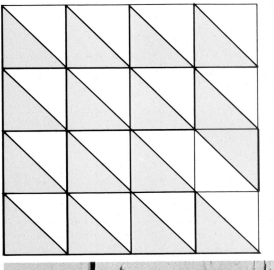 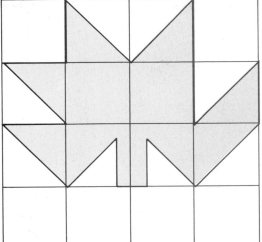

easiest way to do this is to join the triangles into squares, the squares into rows and the rows into blocks. Join the patches by machine or by hand: if by machine, sew from edge to edge and press seams open, if by hand, sew along the marked line only, using a small running stitch and backstitching at either end, and press seams to one side.

▨ When you have made the patchwork blocks, cut 13 plain squares from calico, to the same size as the blocks. Place blocks and squares flat on a large surface in the correct order, and stitch them together in vertical rows. Join rows to complete the patchwork.

▨ Cut a backing piece and padding (if you intend to quilt the work) to the size of the finished patchwork. Pin and tack together. If quilting, work running stitch by hand along the lines of the design,

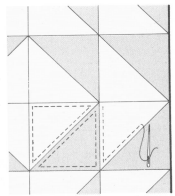

making sure that the needle passes through all layers.

▨ For the border, cut four strips of denim the length of the patchwork plus twice the border width and seam allowances by twice the border width plus seam allowances.

▨ Miter the border ends: fold each strip in half lengthways and bring the two corners at either end up to meet at the fold. Press and cut along the creased line. Place the ends with right sides together; pin and stitch to within ⅝in (1.5cm) of edges. Trim and turn to right side, pushing out the mitered corners. Pin and stitch one edge of border to patchwork; turn under remaining edge of border and stitch to wrong side of patchwork.

INDIAN MAGIC

Traditional patchwork techniques are here combined with richly patterned paisley prints, a type of fabric design which originated in India. The result is a collection of cushions and covers which create a warm and luxurious ambience, and which would bring a touch of Indian summer to a cold, north-facing room even in the depths of winter. The patches are all sewn on to a foundation square as they are joined together, making the finished pieces practical and hardwearing as well as attractive to look at.

MATERIALS

ALL COVERS AND CUSHIONS
Assorted patchwork fabrics –
   plain and patterned fabrics,
   either cottons or silks
Foundation fabric – a firm cotton

would be ideal
Colored pencils
Matching threads

In addition you will need:

BED SQUARE
Ribbons for patchwork

LOG CABIN TABLECLOTH
3¼yd (3m) of 36in (90cm) wide
   fabric for backing
1⅝yd (1.5m) of suitable fabric for
   border

10in (25cm) square of red fabric
Graph paper
Thin card
Long ruler

OBLONG CUSHION
¾yd (60cm) of 36in (90cm) wide
   fabric for cushion back
13in (33cm) zipper
2¾yd (2.4m) edging cord

4 tassels
24in × 20in (60cm × 50cm)
   cushion pad

OCTAGONAL CUSHION
Ribbons for patchwork
¾yd (60cm) of 36in (90cm) wide
   fabric for cushion back
12in (30cm) zipper

1⅓yd (1.2m) of 36in (90cm) wide
   plain cotton fabric for cushion
   pad
Suitable filling

DIRECTIONS

THE BED SQUARE

▦ Cut out and make up (if necessary) a foundation square measuring 63in (160cm). Mark the center of the square with tacking stitches from corner to corner.

▦ For the center, cut out one 13¾in (35cm) square (1), adding ¼in (6mm) seam allowance all round. Place right side up at center of foundation square, as shown. Pin and stitch in place.

▦ Cut four isosceles triangles (2) with two sides 10in (25cm) long and one side 13¾in (35cm), adding seam allowance all around.

Place each triangle wrong side up on square, one by one, matching long edges, pinning and stitching and then turning the triangle over to lie right side up.

▦ Cut four isosceles triangles (3) with two sides 13¾in (35cm) and one side 50cm (20in), plus seam allowances, and apply in the same way.

▦ Cut two strips (4) to the length of the patchwork and 3in (8cm) wide and apply to two facing sides of the patchwork square. Cut two strips the same width and the length of the patchwork plus border strips, and apply to the two remaining sides.

Western patchwork and Indian patterns

▣ Cut four isosceles triangles (5) with two sides of 31in (77cm), divided by a right angle, and apply them to the patchwork as shown.

▣ Cut four border strips (6) measuring 63in × 4in (160cm × 10cm). Attach the top and bottom strips along the inside edge, stopping 3¾in (9.5cm) short of the edge at either side. Apply the side strips in the same manner and then trim and turn under the ends of the top and bottom strips and turn under to form a miter Pin.

▣ Turn in the raw edges of the border and the foundation fabric to meet each other around the outside and either topstitch or slipstitch in place. Slipstitch miters.

▣ Cut four strips of 2¼in (5.5cm) wide ribbon (7) to the length of the center square and apply them, mitering the corners as with the outer border.

▣ Cut four strips of ⅝in (1.5cm) wide ribbon (8) and apply as shown to the second square, using the same technique.

THE LOG CABIN TABLECLOTH

▣ From the foundation fabric, cut out four 25in (65cm) squares. Mark the center with tacking stitches, from corner to corner.

▣ Make each square in the same way: from red fabric, cut one 4in (10cm) square (A), adding ¼in (6mm) seam allowance all around. Pin the fabric square right side up centrally over the foundation square. Handstitch in place along the seamline.

▣ Divide your fabrics into two groups – plains and patterns. Cut the fabrics into strips: take a long ruler and colored pencil and mark strips 2½in (6.2cm) wide across the fabric width, then cut out.

▣ Take a plain strip (B) and trim to the length of the center square. Place face down on square, matching edges, and pin and stitch. Fold strip back to the right side. Take a second plain strip (C); trim to length of A plus B and apply in the same way as before.

▣ Continue in the same way, taking the next two strips from the patterned pile and working on round the square. Strips B, C, F and G should be plain, and strips D, E, H and I patterned. After the

last round, tack the free edges to the foundation square.

▣ Join the four squares along the patterned edges, so that the plain sides lie at the corners.

▣ Cut four border strips 56½in (144cm) × 4in (10cm) wide. Lay the top and bottom strips face down on the edge of the patchwork and, still taking a ¼in (6mm) seam allowance, stitch the strips to the patchwork, stopping ¼in (6mm) short of the edge of the patchwork at either side and leaving an equal amount overlapping. Join the two remaining strips in the same way. Miter the corners.

▣ Make up backing fabric to the same size.

▣ Place patchwork and backing with right sides together and machine round the edges, taking a ⅝in (1.5cm) allowance and leaving an opening for turning. Turn and slipstitch opening.

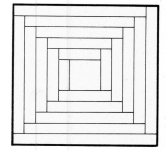

THE OBLONG CUSHION

▦ From fabric cut out the cushion background (1) 24¾in × 21in (63cm × 53cm). Mark the center both ways with tacking stitches. From fabric cut out the central lozenge (2) with 9½in (24cm) and 8in (20cm) diagonals, adding allowance all round of ¼in (6mm). Place right side up centrally on the background; pin and stitch.

▦ Make up a long strip of fabric 43¾in × 5in (111cm × 12.5cm). Cut a length of 1½in (4cm) wide ribbon to the same length. Place ribbon centrally on right side of fabric strip; pin and stitch in place. From this made-up strip cut four trapezoids (3) with 14in (37cm) and 6¼in (16cm) long edges, plus allowance. Pin and stitch together across the diagonal edges. Turn under the seam allowance on remaining edges and place on background. Pin and stitch in place.

▦ From fabric cut out a lozenge (4) with diagonals of 4¼in (11cm) and 3½in (9cm), adding allowance. Turn under allowance and place over center. Pin and stitch in place.

▦ Apply ribbon (5) around the outer edge of the made-up center as for the bed square.

▦ For the four corners (6), from fabric cut out four isosceles triangles with two 4¾in (12cm) sides, divided by a right angle, adding seam allowances all around. Turn under base edge and place to each corner of background. Pin and stitch in place.

▦ For the cushion back, cut out two pieces of fabric, each 24¼ × 11in (63cm × 28cm). Place backs with right sides together; along one long side, pin and stitch in from outer edges for 6in (15cm), taking a ⅝in (1.5cm) seam allowance. Pin and stitch a zipper into the central opening. Open zipper. Place back to patchwork front with right sides together; pin and stitch all around, taking ⅝in (1.5cm) seam allowance. Trim and turn to right side.

▦ Handstitch cord all around the outer edge of the cushion along the seamline. Stitch a tassel to each corner. Insert cushion pad; close zipper.

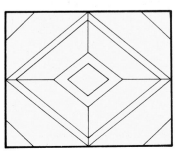

THE OCTAGONAL CUSHION

▦ From fabric cut out a 23½in (60cm) foundation square. Mark the center both ways with tacking stitches. Tack an outline of a square (4) with 5½in (14cm) long sides.

▦ Make up 5½in (14cm) squares (2) (plus allowance) by joining strips of fabric together. In the same way, make up isosceles triangles (3) with 5½in (14cm) long sides, divided by a right angle.

▦ Pin and stitch the squares and triangles together as shown in the diagram. Place on foundation square surrounding marked central square. Turn under inner and outer edges; pin and stitch.

▦ Make up the central square (4) from four isosceles triangles with a 6¾in (17cm) base and 4½in (11.5cm) sides (plus allowances). Each triangle is made up from rows of ribbon and fabric. Position on the foundation square diagonally over the center; turn under the outer edge; pin and stitch in place.

The complicated effect is achieved by stitching together strips of fabric and ribbon and then stitching the resulting bands together. The exception is the central square where all the seams match.

▦ Trim down foundation square in line with the patchwork. For the border, cut a length of fabric 63in × 2¾in (160cm × 7cm) plus allowance. Pin and stitch together into a ring. Pin and stitch around the central octagon, making small pleats at each corner.

▦ For back of cushion cover, cut two pieces to the size of half the patchwork and border, plus a ⅝in (1.5cm) allowance along the long edge. Join along long edge, leaving a 12in (30cm) gap for the zipper at the center. Tack along seam; pin, tack and stitch zipper.

▦ With right sides together, join cushion back to front and turn out through zipper opening.

▦ From plain cotton, make cushion pad to the same size as cover, fill with stuffing and close. Insert pad into cover.

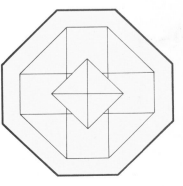